SHAWARMA

Emad Blake

This edition first published in paperback by
Michael Terence Publishing in 2024
www.mtp.agency

Copyright © 2024 Emad Blake

Emad Blake has asserted the right to be identified as
the author of this work in accordance with the
Copyright, Designs and Patents Act 1988

ISBN 9781800948914

No part of this publication may be reproduced, stored
in a retrieval system, or transmitted, in any form or
by any means, electronic, mechanical, photocopying,
recording or otherwise, without the prior
permission of the publisher

Cover design (AI)
2024 Michael Terence Publishing

Michael Terence
Publishing

To you, my father, may God's mercy be upon you.
Your life's struggle feeds me with hope
to face the pains of time.

Your son,
Emadeldin

I forget the taste of warm tea,
I forget the cold of the wind when it blows.
So don't stop without doing anything,
And revive those good memories of me.

From contemporary Turkish poetry

1
The train and the wind

My son, this story is for you, and I am sure you will love it very much. It is a story about your father's long struggle in life, and the fruit of that struggle was you. You will know everything at the right time, and I ask you to listen to me carefully. I know you will be a good listener, and no one can tell you about what happened better than I can. However, if this true tale needs to be written in a book one day, no one would be better suited for the task than your aunt. She promised to do it with love and dedication, ensuring it is done in the best possible way. You will learn who she is at the right time; although she is not really your aunt by blood, as you are Sudanese and she is Turkish, she still deserves that title because she has earned it.

Anyhow, the boy who was me looked at his distant dreams from the top of the train, believing that one day he would become something very important when the sky would open its doors despite any obstacles. He had a great sense of that, a feeling that seemed to cover his heart, as nothing else occupied his mind but looking at the clouds while the train ran in front of them in the opposite direction. They were in the sky, and he was on the ground, but I was on the roof of the train, escaping from paying for the ticket because I hadn't bought one. How could a poor boy afford ten pounds? And most importantly, I wasn't doing anything forbidden; there were many like me, including some elderly people, travelling on top of the train cars without paying anything to the owners.

'This train is owned by the government, my son.'

Said an old man who was sitting close to me. The cold wind of February was hitting his body, but he was better off than I was, as he covered his face with a cotton scarf. Only his small eyes, a very small nose, and the contours of his small cheeks were barely visible.

He was silent for a while before he lit a poor-quality cigarette called Abu-Nakhla, which had a palm tree with four orange heads on the back of the packet. It was the same kind of cigarette my father used to smoke when he came home drunk at midnight and started to hit my mother, waking up everyone in the neighbourhood.

'Travelling on top of the train is exciting, and the best part is that it's free. Tell me, what is your name, boy?'

The man spoke again.

I told him my name. My voice was low, and it seemed that the man didn't hear me due to the wind, or perhaps his ears were weary from the pains of age. To make sure he heard me, he leaned his right ear closer to me, and he tilted, puffing cigarette smoke into my face unintentionally.

'Tell me who is your name, boy.'

He repeated the question.

I told him again, shouting loudly so he could hear me clearly. As my voice rose, the cold winter wind rushed to catch it.

Where does the wind carry people's voices? I wondered how the wind swallowed all these loud shouts and laughter from the people on top of the train. And where does it take them?

As far as the eye could see, the length of the long train was filled with people eating, laughing, chatting, smoking, and doing everything else. The top of the train was like a neighbourhood between the ground and the sky.

'The state's money is permissible, my son. This train was bought with our rights.'

After the old man knew my name, he turned to tell me, while I focused on listening to what he was saying.

He started to say a lot of words with no value to me or I could understand, His voice came and went with the wind which became much stronger. He came with words like president, ministers, farmers, merchants. He was talking about thefts, corruption, games, and conspiracies hatched in the dark.

That last image took me back to when my father would enter our house at midnight, in complete darkness due to the lack of electricity in our home and the entire town for a long time. There wasn't a single lit lamp in any house or on the street. The only exception was a large house located near the river, between the bean fields and the local government offices where my father worked as a driver. This grand and elegant two-story house was the only one with lights on day and night, as no one ever turned them off.

The loud sound of a generator became very clear at night, given the town's silence, except for the noise coming from our house after my father's arrival. He would start his nightly routine, which made it difficult for us to rest.

The old man continued his chatter, his voice coming and going, while I started to feel tired from the cold and my frail body began to tremble, especially since I was wearing only a light tourist and shirt with no underwear. I thought the old man would be generous and lend me his scarf to protect me, as it is customary for elders to be kind to the younger ones. However, this did not happen. I saw no empathy from him despite his frequent phrases about a strange disease affecting people in the town, which he called envy or selfishness. He concluded by summarizing his remarks:

'The weak of faith, the lack of faith, my son.'

He repeated the words, the remarkable discovery he claimed was responsible for all the misfortune and unhappiness related to that mysterious thing he called the nation, of which both he and I were a part. This understanding came to me from the words swallowed by the wind.

I was on the verge of dying from the cold, but God took care of me when a boy, much like myself, came walking on top of the train, holding a tea kettle and pouring tea for the passengers on the roof. He put the coins he received into his pocket. He had a large pocket in the middle of a dirty Damour cloth, tied around his shoulders with a thick rope.

I know that tea reduces the sensation of cold, and my mother used it as a weapon to warm our little bodies during the winter holidays. We would sit under the sun in our house in the early morning hours until the morning was fully bright before my father would sometimes come in to ask for breakfast—and with him, the hell would come into the house.

I didn't have money, as I told you, my son, so I had to pay for the ticket and travel inside the train. Unlike my miserable father, I value honesty.

Fortunately, I found some coins that I hadn't thought were valuable, forgotten in my trousers pocket. I took them out, counted them, and realised they were enough to pay for two cups of tea—the second one went for the old man who thanked me profusely.

I didn't know if he had any money with him or not, so that he could have paid before me. But the important thing was that he lifted his arms high towards the sky, whispering words I couldn't hear. I understood that he was praying for me. As his scarf slipped slightly off his shoulder, I could see part of his face and the top of his head. His hair was completely white, and lice were falling from it, clearly visible against the stark white background.

I realised that I was observing the black lice wandering through the alleys of his white hair. He glanced at me as he lit another cigarette and said, 'This is their home, my son. I will not expel them from their home.'

I, too, had a head full of lice just two years ago. My mother would take my brothers and me to sit under the sun while she washed our heads with gasoline. She had heard from the women in the neighbourhood that this was the best way to get rid of this disaster. Despite all her efforts, there was no progress until the lice decided on their own to leave my head.

The train was about to enter a station for a stop, so the passengers on the roof began hurrying down, trying to escape the railway police who could catch them for violating the regulations. I followed their lead, though it required skills and tricks that I had no experience with before. I watched what they were doing and tried to imitate them.

The old man hurried down between two carriages with a surprising agility that didn't match his age. He skilfully maneuverer through the narrow space where the two cars were connected and then slipped inside the train. I managed to do the same, finding myself squeezed among a large group of people—men, women, and children. At the back, there seemed to be one of the train's dirtiest toilets, as the foul smell hit me strongly. I had to cope with the situation, waiting for the train to stop shaking so that everyone inside could step out and breathe fresh air.

I got off the carriage onto the station platform. All the stations had a uniform rhythm from the time they were built over a century ago by the English during their colonial rule. The small huts with their pyramid-rounded-up shaped roofs gave the stations a unique architectural style.

The old man was nearby but didn't follow me. I was very hungry and didn't have money for food. There were vendors selling sandwiches made from Egyptian beans, falafel, boiled eggs, and also tea and juices despite the cold weather—though the drinks were served with hot water. The smell of grilling beef wafted from a man sitting on a small bench with a large pan in front of him, tossing pieces of meat into hot oil. Those with enough money gathered around him, especially as the smell of the meat was particularly tempting in the cold weather.

    I could only smell the food until the train whistled, so I hurriedly climbed to the roof of the train, but I couldn't find my elderly friend. He had disappeared from view, and I started scanning the roofs from south to north in search of him. The crowd was so dense that it was difficult to distinguish between people or find the old man amid the sheer number of them. Despite my best efforts, I wasn't able to locate him. I didn't know where he had gone! Eventually, I decided to give up searching, but then I remembered that he had left a small knapsack with me while I was standing near the meat vendor. The bag was still in my hand, but how could I return it to him if I couldn't find him? I decided to wait for the next station, hoping that he was also searching for me and that we would meet again.

    I thought about walking on top of the cars, going back and forth in search of the old man, but it seemed very difficult due to the cold wind and the crowd. The risk of falling was high, especially if the train started moving faster than its initial slow lazy speed. I looked around and saw some passengers sleeping cross-legged. How could anyone sleep in such a precarious place? The narrow width of the carriage made it risky, with the potential to fall and be seriously injured or worse. I had heard many stories of people falling from the tops of trains because they had made the mistake of trying to sleep there. I knew I had to stay alert for the rest of the journey, though I had no idea where it would take me.

I decided to escape from our house that miserable evening when my father came home early, which was unusual. He began his routine of harshly beating my mother until she stumbled and fell to the ground. When my brothers and I tried to help her get up, my father turned on us, lashing our backs with his whip. I had five brothers and nine sisters, and we all suffered under his brutality.

I was thirteen years old at the time. Beneath me, there were five younger brothers and three sisters, the youngest of whom was a toddler who hadn't yet celebrated her first birthday and wasn't spared from the beatings. My mother was in a constant state of pregnancy—giving birth only to become pregnant again almost immediately, as my father never gave her a chance to recover.

After he finished beating her each night, he would then fall on top of her in whatever position, indifferent to our presence and feelings. He would proceed to have sex in front of us, completely ignoring the suffering he was causing his children. His drunken state rendered him oblivious to our pain. Despite his intoxication, his physical strength was still formidable, allowing him to overpower anyone who crossed his path.

It was a shame to have a father like this. At school, in the street, at the market, in neighbourhood alleys—everywhere, people knew us as the children of that cruel. strange man. Our house was infamous for its constant weeping at night and the shouting at any time of day. The behaviour of the household reflected on all of us, leading to constant fighting, anger, and commotion over trivial matters. Violence was a norm in our home, and carrying knives was commonplace. One of my older brothers would often chase younger siblings, both boys and girls, with a knife. This became a daily occurrence, as did taking someone to the hospital for severe bleeding.

I vividly remember one time when my older brother hit one of my younger sisters and cut between her buttocks. It was an incredibly painful and disturbing scene for me. I still feel the pain and disgust when I recall it, seeing the dark blood flowing from under her.

I was nearly the only one who remained unaffected by the chaos of our household—by the knives, shouting, and rough behaviour. The people in the neighbourhood saw me as an exception, and they often commented on this in front of me. There was nothing hidden about our family's misdeeds; everyone was aware of them. People were curious about how I managed to be respectful and decent despite growing up in such a troubled environment and a strange house.

I myself didn't fully understand the reason. I believed it was a choice made by God, that I was meant to be different in order to escape the hell of my upbringing and find a better life elsewhere. And that's exactly what happened.

On the same day I escaped, I left behind all my hopes and dreams tied to my family and the town where I was born and spent my early childhood. Among the things I left behind was my academic excellence. I had been the top student at school, which was another miracle of distinction in a family marked by madness and chaos, as even the teachers had openly remarked.

Nothing was hidden in that house. My father used to a recognised daily program that started from the early morning. Despite his late sleeping he was used to wake up early even if he just sleeps for two hours. He had an extra power but he used it in nonsense things and in bashing us and threatening our mother, our life.

The first thing he did each morning was to start the engine of the government car, an old, earthy-coloured Land Rover with a rear storage compartment. Before leaving, he would insert a plastic hose into the car's fuel tank, then suck on the hose to siphon gasoline into a plastic bottle, spitting out the initial mouthful before filling the bottle halfway. He did this every day to have fuel ready for sale.

At precisely ten in the morning, a man would arrive—never late—to take the gasoline and hand a few pounds to my mother. She couldn't spend a single penny of it, as she had to hand over the full amount to my father. If she even thought of spending just one pound, she knew what her fate would be. Regardless, she couldn't avoid the beating that awaited her each night.

My father worked as a driver for the local governor, who owned the two-story house where he lived, a house that never lacked electricity. The governor was fond of my father and often gave him extra money, which my father squandered on his personal indulgences. He never had to worry about being fired or having his salary cut. I often saw him in the governor's office and home, humbly bowing his head, especially in front of the governor's wife when he delivered vegetables, meat, and bread to her in the morning. She was always astonished by the rumours in the neighbourhood about my father being a strange man.

One day, the lady asked me, 'Is it true that he hits your mother?'

I found her question impolite. I looked at her but didn't answer. She understood that I wasn't pleased with what she said. No matter what happened, he was still my father, she was my mother, and this was our home.

That night when I escaped, my father had decided to expel all of us from the house. He was drunk, as usual, and he often made these threats. Typically, we'd spend half the night on the street or with sympathetic neighbours, only to return later and carry on as if nothing had happened. But this time, it felt different. Midnight had passed, and nothing had changed—we didn't see our mother coming to take us back home, nor did we hear our father's voice calling us in the dark.

My mind was working in a strange way that night; I felt a deep urge to leave this place, especially that house. I told myself that I couldn't continue living there. I had to escape and find a new life somewhere else. Where exactly? I didn't know, and I had no clear plan. The most important thing was to follow what my imagination was telling me.

There was nothing in my mind only to forget the past. I decided with myself that I would go to the capital of the country at the south of our town as there are chances for life that what I heard from people. Surely I could find a job to tackle my things, and the most important that I would get rid off the continuous paining from this daily modeness.

The train was about to enter the station in our town, which wasn't far from our house—less than a kilometer — and I knew I could reach it in time. As I had guessed, I arrived just as the train began to move, and I sat next to my friend, the old man. Gradually, the cars' shaking subsided, and the train's speed increased. My mind was set on one thing: forgetting the past. I decided that I would go to the capital city, located south of our town, where I had heard there were better opportunities. Surely, I could find a job there and start sorting out my life. Most importantly, I would finally escape the endless distress that had been causing me so much pain.

I even forgot about my academic success in school—what could I do with it? Sooner or later, I would leave it behind for some uncertain reason. This same pattern had repeated with my brothers, and staying in this environment meant that one day I might lose my resilience too. I learned a hard lesson from my older brother, who, like me, had been successful in school and was always polite. But one day, after enduring too much harassment from my father, he lost his patience. He ended up grabbing a knife, threatening the family, and eventually became a drunkard like our father, spending his days doing nothing but chasing girls in the neighbourhood. I wouldn't let my life follow the same path. That was my vow to myself as I sat on top of the train.

The thought of escaping wasn't new to me; it had been swirling in my mind from time to time, especially as I constantly felt out of place in this house. My father continued with his harmful behaviour, and my mother chose painful neutrality, doing nothing. I knew she was suffering, but she seemed incapable of anything other than distancing herself for the sake of peace, as she always said. To her, that meant enduring this torment to keep the family together. But I wondered, what house was she talking about? Was it this house, this family, or something else entirely?

The train had approached the large station after travelling hundreds of kilometers, on a journey that remains etched in my mind to this day. It was a fateful journey with unknown outcomes for a boy who dreamed of finding himself far from the hell he had known.

The train passed through dozens of stations, and with each one, I discovered the vastness of our country. It was my first time travelling beyond my town. I saw a variety of scenes: an expansive desert stretching to the far horizon, where it seemed to touch the sky in every direction; a river running beside the railway but in the opposite direction, disappearing and reappearing again; green fields interspersed with parched land; nomads tending their camels on patches of newly sprouted grass; scattered pyramids with broken tips as if they had fallen from a distant planet; and small cars stuck in the sand, with men pulling them out using ropes.

This is my country, but only a small part of it—not even a quarter of its vastness. From what I learned in geography class, our country spans a million square miles, yet we are still poor. They say forests are covering the far south—will I ever get to see them one day? I wondered as my mind drifted through my fragmented imagination. I had no idea what my fate would be or what was going to happen to me.

We entered the capital, the big city. I recognised it by the tall buildings rising on the horizon, the heavy traffic, the crowded streets, and the smoke billowing everywhere. From the start, life here felt different and unique, nothing like what I was used to in our northern town. There, the only large building was the house occupied by the local governor. We didn't have paved streets like the ones here, but the air in our town was much fresher—you never felt suffocated. Everyone knew each other, and if someone did something wrong, the news would spread quickly. Here, everything felt different, and the people seemed as if they were living in a constant state of chaos, like a scene from doomsday.

Everyone was talking to themselves as they ran, though I couldn't understand why. From my vantage point on the roof of the train, I observed the commotion, comparing the life back home with the reality of this journey. As soon as the train neared a station, a semblance of normalcy would return. The passengers on the roof, like me, scrambled down into the carriages, hastily avoiding the police who began chasing after us. In the rush, people tumbled over one another, and some were caught. I'd witnessed this scene play out at several stations before, and fortunately, I wouldn't arrested.

My imitation of the old man, whom I followed like a shadow, had been the key to my survival in times past. But now, where was he? He had vanished at the station before the last one. I only realised we were on the edge of the big city from the murmurs and sighs of the passengers. Everyone was gathering their belongings and memories from the roof of the train, preparing for an uncertain future. Like me, many had no idea what awaited us. I glanced around and noticed that there was no one my age; they were all older, the youngest seeming to be in his early twenties. I told myself to hurry and leave the top of the train. My guide to survival this time would be the skills I had learned from the old man.

As I was squeezing my left foot into the flexible space between two train cars, dangling hastily while everyone around me hurried to get off, a strong hand grabbed me from below and pulled me like a rope tied to a stone. I felt my body spin in the air at least three times before I hit the ground, while another man, different from the one who had grabbed me, pressed a huge boot on my back. I couldn't see anything above me as my head was crushed against the cold tiles of the station floor. Out of the corner of my right eye, struggling to turn my head with great difficulty, I saw the train policeman stepping on me without mercy, as my breath grew shallow and I felt a crushing tightness, thinking I was about to die on the spot.

It was a harsh welcome. I got up, only to be escorted to a small office with a barred cell behind it. The space was cramped, and I soon discovered I wasn't alone—there were dozens of others like me who had been caught, which reassured me somewhat. As long as you're with people, you won't feel isolated. The important thing is that they are decent and respectable, like the old man I had met earlier, even if they were a bit stingy. Hunger had completely consumed me, my stomach aching, with no relief in sight until the group ahead of me in line finished their interrogation. What would happen to me afterward… only God knew.

I was the only boy among the violators of travel regulations. There were no women, only men. I felt proud that I had become a man, punished for a crime against the law for the first time in my life. I heard one of them cursing and swearing, indifferent to the policemen or the lieutenant, as indicated by the insignia on his shoulder. The man was shouting, 'It's a badge of honour for any human being to stand against the law in this country.' Others were silent, while two men muttered in agreement, their voices low but audible to the policeman guarding the line, who was holding a whip and began striking those who tried to cause a commotion after the man's outburst. There was some confusion, then things quieted down again with the sound of the whip on bodies. I didn't escape the beating. The image of my father beating my mother and us flashed before my eyes with each lash on my frail body from the soldier, who seemed to resemble my father as if they had been cast in the same mould. He had a thick moustache, a clean-shaven face, a sagging belly like the plains the train had crossed. He held a cigarette in one hand, puffing away while he beat with the other, relishing his action.

'We'll let you go if you pay for the ticket… out of kindness due to your young age'

The officer said to me when I stood before him.

'But I don't have any money,' I replied.

He looked at the old man's bag… still with me. I didn't know how I managed to keep it throughout everything that had happened. It hadn't been lost in all the commotion I had endured.

'What do you have with you?'

He said, pointing to the bag.

'I don't know!'

He was surprised by my response; it was clear from the expression on his broad, furrowed forehead. He got up from his seat, stood in front of me, and forcefully took the bag, emptying its contents onto the table. First, an old Quran fell out, followed by a locally made prayer beads from the fruits of the lalob tree… but a small one, not the long kind that dervishes wear in nightly remembrance circles as they lose themselves in love for the Prophet. Then, a bundle of banknotes tumbled out. That was a surprise I hadn't expected. It was a large sum, it seemed—perhaps a thousand pounds, as each note was ten pounds. I think there were a hundred notes in total.

The officer slammed his hands on the table, astonished by the large amount of money, but not more shocked than I was. Was the old man carrying all this money and yet didn't pay for a cup of tea… or buy food for himself or for me, despite seeing me shivering repeatedly from the cold and hunger? I doubt he didn't understand that I was hungry. The officer interrupted my thoughts, asking me:

'Is this money yours?'

'No… it's not mine, sir!'

'Then you stole it… You must be a thief.'

He didn't let me answer. He was hurling accusations and insults without mercy. The scene wasn't unfamiliar to me; our house in the town was near the police station, and I often witnessed battles in front of the station between thieves and criminals being caught and the officers. It sometimes made me feel as though they were all criminals. Now I was in the position of the criminal, with no defence. What was I to do?

I tried to explain to him that the whole story… that there was an old man who was with me on the train roof… that the man was… that I was following him… that he handed me the bag, and I hadn't seen him since… that he must have been disappointed in me and probably thought of me as a thief just as the officer was accusing me now. The truth was, I couldn't speak or clarify; I was still a child, with no great means to confront the adult world. I kept silent, realizing the officer wasn't interested in understanding me; his eyes were only on the money. I wasn't too young to know that 'people die for money… they don't care about the means, as long as the money is in front of them', as I'd heard my mother say often.

The officer took me aside to another office. There was a small door in the narrow room I hadn't noticed before. We entered through it, and there was a higher-ranking officer sitting behind the desk, his face hidden behind a newspaper. He set it aside as he listened to the lieutenant report that they had caught the youngest criminal on the train. The man looked at me; he seemed polite, unlike his colleague, and asked me:

'Where did you learn to steal... you seem to be from a faraway place?'

'I'm not a thief, sir... I swear to God I didn't steal it... the story is...'

I told to him whole story as I had just narrated it. The man listened to me without interrupting, which gave me a temporary sense of relief. When I finished, he calmly gestured to the lieutenant to set the money aside on the table, return the Quran and prayer beads to the bag, and hand it back to me and he then said:

'Go, boy, and don't let it happen again'

There was no way I could convince him that the money wasn't mine, that the old man was certainly waiting for me somewhere outside the station, and that he would ask me about the money. No matter what I said, he wouldn't believe me. He would accuse me of theft. There was no room for any other conversation. So, I took the bag and left while the men in line watched me, some seeing me as a thief, others thinking I had been deceived, some feeling pity for me, and others not caring at all. I left through the iron door, bidding farewell to the narrow hall with the last lash on my back from the second version of my father.

I carried the bag in my hand, after the money had been stolen from it in broad daylight. Now, I understood why the old man was grumbling about the situation in the country, talking about corruption, thefts, and people taking money unjustly, and his theory about the weakness of faith. Those two officers were embodiments of what he was talking about. They weren't just weak in faith—they had no faith at all. I spat on the ground, my stomach still hurting. I had no specific destination other than having reached the big city, my goal. From there, I would think about the rest of the journey. And If I had been thinking before of finding the old man to return his bag to him, I abandoned that goal now, fearing that he might see me as a suspect. He might be looking for me at the station, so I quickly needed to leave the area, head to nearby streets, and then take a long road that led me to a crowded area full of people.

There were signs everywhere—street names, shop addresses, pharmacies, barbershops, bakeries, bookstores, and restaurants reminding me of my hunger. There were street vendors selling everything imaginable and unimaginable. Some spread used books on the ground; others were begging. Blind women walked and begged, disabled people dragged their sticks while bickering, young girls and older women displayed their charms in tight clothes that revealed almost everything. Boys in loose, patterned shirts and others with colourful leather bags and curly hair hanging back. Homeless boys chased trash in large dumpsters, modern cars, and dilapidated ones making annoying noises, and a traffic policeman standing on a high platform at the intersection, raising his hand and whistling loudly, puffing his cheeks as much as possible.

It was a fascinating world for me, seeing this human theatre before me, but I was more preoccupied with my hunger and confusion about the coming hours. My vision was blurred, and my body was exhausted.

My mother often told us about her older brother who lived in this big city, whom I had seen for the first time on television at the local governor's house when I occasionally went with my father. She said he worked as the manager of the big bank in the city.

She would tell us, in scattered moments, about their childhood—she was a few years younger, perhaps five at most. They had other siblings, but they had dispersed across the country and abroad. She had little ongoing contact with them; we rarely saw them or knew them well. Once, when our old grandmother died in a village near the town west of the river, most of them came. They drove big four-wheel-drive cars, wore distinctive white turbans, and bright clothes, with forced smiles on their faces. We were introduced to them. 'This is your uncle, this is your aunt', and so on. They left the next day after burying their mother. That was perhaps seven years ago. I vaguely remember them; it's hard to recall their faces if I saw any of them again. That was the second time I saw my uncle, but this time in person, not on the screen.

I thought about looking for him, my uncle, hoping he could help me escape my past. My mother said that despite everything, he remained a good man, generous and helpful to those who came to his house. Once, she travelled to the capital, taking one of my younger siblings, and returned with a large collection of gifts, clothes, and toys, saying that my uncle had bought them for us.

My father didn't like hearing about my mother's brothers, whether in praise or criticism. Whenever she tried to defend them for their absence, she would get a beating with the long whip my father hung in the big room of our house, which was the only one we had besides a small kitchen in a distant corner. She would get a severe beating from the whip that no one dared touch or move from its place, as many in the house would volunteer information as soon as the executioner arrived.

All I knew was that the big bank was where I could find my uncle. If I could get there, I would definitely find him. I had nothing to lose; I would reach him, and he would take care of me. I didn't think my mother was lying about him. Due to his busy schedule and his government position, he didn't have enough time to care for others. His mere dedication to his important work served everyone, she used to say, but she used to say this away from my father's hearing. Once, she said he loved anyone who excelled in school and succeeded, as he had been a top student and studied at the country's top university, at a time when going to university was a miracle.

For all that, my mother used to say, so I had the motivations to think of him as my primary goal in the city. Perhaps I would find rest and comfort in his house, and if he knew about my academic excellence and that I was the top student in school, he might help me continue my education. I daydreamed—did he have children or daughters my age? Would I grow up and marry one of his daughters? That was premature, and I didn't remember my mother telling us anything about the number or ages of his children. She only talked about him, saying he was fine, but she sometimes complained about his wife, saying she was tough on strangers, though he controlled the house, and that was what mattered.

I resisted my growing hunger. The sun had come out, dispersing the clouds after mid-morning, reducing the chill in the air, especially as the dense movement of people created noticeable warmth in the area. As the noon call to prayer echoed from a large, tall, and magnificent mosque like I had never seen before, I reached a busier street with more people and cars moving slowly among them. I still carried the bag that had hurt my hand, but I decided to keep it, just in case the old man appeared. I clung to it as a sign of my honesty, even though it would be incomplete evidence.

Once my goal was set to reach the big bank before 3 p.m., when businesses in the country closed, my random wandering through the streets became more organized. Before that, I had no specific route.

I sought help from passersby, asking this person, that one, and another. Everyone provided some information. The question I might have asked for the twentieth time: How do I get to the big bank?

Unlike in our town, no one cared much about you when you asked for a specific location. There, everyone volunteered to answer your question, and dozens might accompany you to your destination. That doesn't happen here. There's no chivalry or pity for a hungry, miserable boy, as my ragged clothes made clear. I realised they had gotten a bit dirty, and my shoes were worn out, possibly about to tear at any moment.

It was an uncalculated adventure by all standards, I told myself, cursing the moment I decided to run away. My father's hell was more bearable. Now, my siblings would have returned home, and the whole story would be over. I had acted too hastily. I should go back, but I needed money. Should I travel again on the train roof?

In moments when one is about to make a brave decision, things happen that change the direction of the wind. That's what happened to me because just as I was about to convince myself to return to the train station, a large sign appeared in front of me with the words 'The Big Bank'. So, this is it. Despite many people laughing at me when I asked, saying there are dozens of big banks here, which bank do you mean, boy?

Shawarma

I was sure because I knew my mother's accuracy; there was only one big bank, while smaller ones followed it or were smaller, like the only bank in our town. But people here don't stop to listen to you or argue like they do there; everyone rushes to their destination.

I stared at the sign, nearly two meters tall and possibly seven, if not ten, meters wide. I couldn't see well due to exhaustion, fatigue, and the burning in my stomach. I was watching it standing solid, her letters carved from marble on the tall, multi-story building. I stared at it as if I had invented, assembled, or conceived the idea. It was like finding a great treasure. That giant sign was my treasure in the big city.

Now the most important, yet easier step, was ahead, after confirming with the guard standing at the wide iron gate that this was the place I sought. My mother was indeed precise in her information. Thank you, God, for giving me a mother who doesn't lie, exaggerate, or understate, even about a cruel and harsh father.

This sign was my salvation, I told myself. The young guard, who seemed to be around my age, stood there with a cheerful smile. This meant they paid him well; otherwise, he wouldn't be smiling all the time. I imagined myself standing there. I didn't want to push him out of his position, but I meant I would forget about school, and my uncle would find me a job in this giant institution.

I saw dozens of people coming in and out, cars parking and others leaving, and large boxes being carried by strong men. It seemed like they were filled with money. I know a little about these things from what I've seen at the town market when they bring one of those boxes to the only bank there, though it's much smaller than these.

I thought to myself that my uncle must rule over this vast kingdom and live in luxury. He must be a very important man in the state. Otherwise, I wouldn't have seen him on the television in the town leader's house years ago, speaking behind a microphone in a grand hall giving a speech that I didn't quite understand. There were many people in that hall, some of them bent over their notebooks, writing down what they heard.

A question crossed my mind, one that I didn't know the answer to: if my uncle is so wealthy and influential, why did he neglect my mother and leave her with my father? Why didn't he help his poor, miserable sister—my mother? I know her misery very well.

The cheerful guard said to me, 'Yes, this is the big bank. Are you looking for someone?'

'My uncle works here. He's the big man here. Can I see him?' I said.

The guard burst out laughing, and I found him quite rude this time. It seems that everyone in this city disappoints me. The senior officer I initially thought would stand up for me took the old man's money instead, proving the exact opposite. And now this young man, who seemed kind, is mocking me. He doesn't believe that a boy like me could have a relative here, let alone the most important man in the place.

He didn't let me stay silent; he said to me, 'You mean His Excellency is your uncle? Why don't you try polishing my shoe, then?'

He lifted his boot high in the air before slamming it down hard on the pavement, laughing loudly as his laughter faded into the cold air amid the street noise. No one here listens to anyone else. Then he yelled at me, 'Get out of here, you vagabond!'

I looked like a real street urchin, and there was no way I could convince him otherwise. I realised that insisting he let me into the building would be useless. So, I decided to step back and find a spot where I could watch the main entrance until my uncle came out. He wouldn't stay there forever, and when he did come out, I would rush to him and call out. But would he recognise me? He had seen me the day my grandmother, his mother, died. I don't think he'll remember me since he didn't stay long—only a day—before leaving. He didn't meet us, my siblings, and me, for more than a few seconds, just long enough for us to line up and greet him. We were a large number, joined by the cousins, and then all the children were ushered away because the man was surrounded by hundreds of people, most of whom had come with personal interests under the guise of condolence—someone looking for a job for their son, or someone seeking financial help for a serious illness, and so on.

He won't remember me, but I'll remember him well because I spent many hours on the day of the funeral spying and observing everything that happened around him while serving water or tea to the mourners. I was one of those boys relied upon for their patience, unlike the others.

Finally, as the workday was nearing its end, I was ready to see him as he headed to the car park. There was a black car, luxurious and distinguished from the other cars, parked in a special spot surrounded by a wire fence, with a green area and flowers around it. Three men were overseeing the washing and polishing of the car. To make sure it belonged to the big boss, I checked the small signs hanging above the parking spaces under the canopies. My assumption was correct; it was written in white on a blue background on a small sign: 'Bank Director's Parking', in both Arabic and English. I read it without needing to get close, to avoid the guard who had spotted me earlier and might come back to chase me away, which would delay my plan.

Time passed slowly. The afternoon prayer call echoed from several mosques, including the grand mosque. I hadn't prayed. I usually make sure to pray, but I hadn't since yesterday. I felt uneasy for neglecting my religious duty. But if I went to pray now, I might miss catching my uncle, who might have stayed late due to some piled-up work. This large building must house hundreds of employees, meaning the man is responsible for every little detail, which surely takes a long time. My mother used to say that sometimes my uncle would come home late for lunch, recounting memories of her trip to visit them. This reassured me that my chances hadn't slipped away and that hope remained.

Just as I was becoming exhausted from hunger, that strange affliction that saps a person's energy, three men quickly approached the black car, opened the doors, and started the engine. They were followed by a tall man in a smart blue suit and a tie, the colour of which I couldn't make out due to my blurred vision from exhaustion. Ahead of him, a short, plump man with a limp walked, carrying a black briefcase. I recognised this man by his distinctive appearance and gait, as he hopped between every two steps. He had come with my uncle on the day of the funeral and had stood by his car at the time, shooing the children away as one would shoo flies from food. The image was clear in my mind—this was my uncle, the tall man with the neatly trimmed beard. Perhaps because on that day seven years ago, he wore a jellabiya and turban, he looked unfamiliar to me at first. I thanked the limping man silently for solving the puzzle for me.

The tall man lit a pipe just as I sprinted towards him, shouting, 'Uncle! Uncle!'

The guard leaped toward me, jumping over the iron fence, while the four men, including the limping man, prepared to punch, probably bewildered at who this wretched person calling out to the director could be. By no stretch of the imagination could it be assumed that his nephew would be in such a shabby state. But it was the truth.

My uncle intervened to resolve the situation, signalling with his right hand for them to step back. Indeed, they moved away from me. He called me to come closer with a broad smile that revealed the features of a kind man. I feared a repeat of my previous experiences, so I decided this time not to trust the first impressions of the meeting. I needed to wait and see what would happen.

The man had recognised me. He even called me by name, saying, 'Come here, don't be afraid. Come.'

He bent close to the ground and planted a kiss on my dirty cheek. I felt its warmth, sensing that a new depth of life would begin to form today. I remembered that my mother had always been precise, as always. She had often said that our uncle was kind and tender-hearted, if not for the circumstances of life that force everyone to take their own path in this world.

My uncle had a photographic memory, as I discovered at that moment and later came to understand even more deeply. He could recall every face in front of him and never forget them. Perhaps it was his work with numbers and accounts, or maybe it was a God-given talent. I found out that he remembered the names of my brothers and sisters and carried a mental image of them. Before understanding how I had arrived here, he asked me:

'Is your mother, okay?'

'She is fine,' I replied.

'Has your father stopped hitting her at night?'

I felt embarrassed that he knew about the beatings, but if the whole town knew, what was strange about him being aware of it? No secret stays hidden. I told him, 'That's why I came here.'

I was honest with him. I felt he wanted to know the truth and that his feelings toward me were noble. He could have forgotten about me, ignored me, or neglected me, but his concern made me feel safe, so I didn't hesitate to tell him the whole story—why I was here!

The black car had started moving, and I was sitting beside him in the back seat. The limping driver was speeding so recklessly that I was scared. I had never ridden in such a spacious, luxurious car in my life, but the speed terrified me. I compared it to my father's rickety car, which he used to bring the daily necessities to the town governor's house every morning. The leader's private car might be special, but it was nothing like this—there was no comparison.

Throughout the journey to my uncle's house, he asked me many questions about how I got there, why I ran away, our situation at home, specifically about my mother, about my father and his continuous cursing, as he described it, and about my siblings, what each one was doing.

He knew that I excelled in school and promised that he would take care of everything. As we prepared to get out when a large gate was opened by an elderly man, and the car stopped inside a wide courtyard surrounded by a green garden with neem trees and climbing plants, my uncle said to me, 'Thank God you got out of that hell. Don't worry.'

So far, things seemed fine. My uncle wouldn't be a replica of the senior officer or the bank guard, who would surely change his opinion of me. He must have been stunned to see me riding next to his boss in the black car. He looked at me in disbelief, almost as if he were watching a movie. In the coming days, when I return to the bank, he'll probably treat me better, and maybe even apologise, and I'll accept his apology.

I snapped out of my daydreams with a light tap on my shoulder from the limping driver. He was playfully tapping me, and seemed much kinder than the way he had attacked me earlier, when he rolled up his sleeves ready to teach me a lesson in manners for being a beggar or a vagabond who should show respect to the upper class. He took out two colourful bottles containing drinks from the car's trunk, handed me one, and gulped down the other in one go without lowering it from his mouth until he finished it. I could hear his burping, while my uncle entered the large house through a door surrounded by flowers.

That delicious drink eased my hunger, and I began to see things more clearly. In front of me was a wide building painted white, with doors in a light blue colour. There was a fountain spilling water into a circular basin in front of us, and to my right, there was a large wire cage with colourful birds, including a cute parrot that was looking at me as if it knew I was new to the place, trying to mimic the way I was holding the refreshing bottle of juice.

2
In my uncle's house

I spent my first night at my uncle's house, but it was filled with harsh dreams, probably due to the feeling of pain and longing for the home I came from, even if life there no longer mattered much to me. What exhausted me the most and made me wake up several times before dawn was the recurring dream of the old man who had accompanied me on the train's roof. He was standing at the final station, waiting for me and asking where my bag was, scolding me for not waiting for him and instead hurriedly fleeing the station without giving himself a chance to listen to me.

The next day, I had the idea to go to the station to look for him, and I actually did so. The limping driver, who had become my friend without much preamble, took me there. I told him what had happened and that I felt guilty. He didn't say much. When I got to the platform, I waited a long time, but no one came. I was just trying to ease my conscience and rid myself of those nightmares.

The second night went smoothly. I had gone to bed early after a long, exhausting day spent waiting. The old man appeared in my dream again, this time thanking me for my efforts, telling me that money didn't matter much to him, and advising me to keep the bag, the Quran, and the prayer beads, as they would bring me good fortune. I felt compelled to follow his advice, as the dream repeated itself several times before dawn. I woke up and went to pray at the nearby mosque. The old guard had opened the gate and walked beside me to the prayer, but he didn't speak to me at all on the way there and back. He just muttered to himself until we neared the house, where he suddenly asked, 'What brought you here?'

Should I tell him my story? Can I trust him? I didn't have an answer. I knew I shouldn't rush into building relationships with people here—that was the limping driver's advice. It's also essential for a person to be clear and not overly polite, as excessive trust in others can backfire. I should have followed this advice with the old man. I thought for a moment before responding with a question:

'What's so strange about me being here?'

The old man wasn't as calm as he initially appeared. Everyone in this city seems to change suddenly. I saw signs of anger on his face as he fumed, saying:

'You're a rude boy…'

His insult made me angry, but I chose to remain composed. I kept silent and made my way to the outer part of the house, to the main guest hall. My uncle was sitting there, apparently having woken up early, reading a book and smoking his pipe. He invited me to sit next to him. I hesitated to tell him what had happened with the guard and decided not to rush. If the insult repeated, I would take action against him. I don't think my uncle would approve of such behaviour.

My initial assessments of many things were incorrect because, over time, things would reveal their true nature. The important thing is that I spent the first few days in the outer part of the house reserved for men, which included that spacious hall where my uncle would sit at dawn to read. He read books on various subjects, mostly in English. I used to be interested in reading in the past, but I never got involved with his books. I was more concerned with figuring out the identities of the people in this place, who each seemed to be a world unto themselves. As I quickly noticed, everyone here lives in their own private world. I didn't need a long time to know that.

In the outer part of the house where I slept, there was a small room with a single window and an iron bed with a soft mattress. There was also an air conditioner, which I didn't need because the weather was cold. In our house, we only have a ceiling fan in the high-ceilinged room where the family gathers. The room here also had a television connected to an external antenna, but it was the old type. I learned that this space was originally reserved for the old guard's son, who lives in the house but is currently away visiting his mother and siblings in their town in the central part of the country. He goes to them with money after several months. I found this out after two days from the limping driver, by chance. This explained the old man's discontent with me and his questioning tone.

Over the next few days, I got to know almost all the household members, unless I missed someone or there are others who might appear in the coming days. There was the old guard, the cook, and the great lady. She was around forty, perhaps a little younger or older—I couldn't tell. I never approached her or greeted her. She was intimidating and formidable, wearing her ornate dresses and strong, locally-made perfume, easily striding in her high heels that made a clattering sound on the tiled courtyard floor. She usually went out in the evenings with my uncle and wouldn't return until late, not before eleven at night. She often yelled and cursed and as soon as she entered the house, with my uncle walking behind her as usual, the walls and trees would shake, and I would feel a chill in my frail body, rushing to hide in my room.

It was difficult for me, while in the room, to figure out what topics sparked her arguments with my uncle, who mostly remained silent. I couldn't understand the reasons for her complaints and raised voice. I wasn't interested in eavesdropping to understand, as curiosity rarely drives me. That night, at the end of the week, they returned even later than usual. Her voice was louder than before. I was sitting in the outer garden with the old man, drinking tea together, which the guard had prepared, and he seemed to be trying to befriend me again without the need to revisit what happened that morning.

Her loud shouting echoed through the still night, and I heard her protesting, saying:

'Do you want to turn this house into a shelter for your bum relatives!'

My uncle didn't respond. As usual, he didn't respond. I had learned his behaviour from previous nights. He tried to speak to say something, but she didn't give him a chance, quickly yelling more and hurling vile insults at my mother, father, my family, and the town I came from. Words like… Ignorant… poor… scoundrels… ungrateful… and more.

The old guard slurped his tea loudly, indifferent to what was happening. I looked at him, trying to ignore the obvious insults I was hearing, while the shouting faded with the sound of high heels until they disappeared into the distant inner part of the house. The guard then turned to me and said:

'If you want to stay here, so you have to get used to this.'

Within two days, my relationship with the old man had strengthened, especially since I had started helping him with tasks related to his work, such as trimming the garden, caring for the birds, or polishing the outer floors after sweeping them. At the same time, the limping driver would come during the day to take me on errands around the city. He would go into many buildings, entering and exiting while I waited in the car without knowing the nature of his business. I thought he was doing work for my uncle related to his job as the manager of the big bank.

However, in his usual way of speaking freely without regard for what he said, as I understood from the beginning, or perhaps he intentionally conveyed certain ideas that were on his mind indirectly... I don't know... he said to me two days after I heard the nighttime insults, as we were returning towards the bank building from several errands he had completed:

'Would you like to work with me?'

I paused for a moment... the idea was good... the schools were closed, which meant I had time to earn some money. Then, if the school season started, I would have something to manage my affairs with. But what would I do with him? I said to him:

'Yes, I really need the money... I don't want my uncle to take care of everything for me'

Suddenly, as if realizing that he shouldn't have brought up the subject, he said to me:

'Let's postpone it... if you need money, I'll give you enough.'

We arrived at the bank. The young guard was standing in his usual spot. He quickly stepped away from the gate to greet us, having extinguished a cigarette he was smoking before finishing it. He seemed a bit nervous and apologised, saying he didn't know who I was the last time. He had been avoiding me in the past days because he was ashamed of himself for doubting my relationship with the manager. The driver responded, saying:

'Go away, you rude person; a thief might come to rob the bank while you play the role of the respectable one.'

The guard didn't reply, walking back to his spot. The limping driver looked at me and said:

'Didn't I tell you? They're all like that... don't trust anyone here.'

The limping driver also handled household tasks, supervising the procurement of vegetables, meat, bread, fruits, and eggs... almost everything. He also directed the old guard and the young cook, who came at the end of the day, did his work in two hours, and placed the food in a large refrigerator in the big kitchen in the outer part of the house, then left. I had no relationship with him, and he didn't care about anything except his work. He was precise in his timing, like a clock. When the limping driver spoke to him, he mostly didn't respond, just nodding his head in agreement, and sometimes I doubted if he heard well.

It was just before noon when we left the bank after about an hour. I didn't enter my uncle's office, as I stayed in a small office where the limping driver kept his belongings. It had only a table, two chairs, and a large picture of the country's president hanging on the wall. I sat there, staring at it, pondering the fate of my coming days until the man returned from his rounds in the offices. His voice seemed to ebb and flow as if carried by a gust of wind, responding arrogantly to some greetings and issuing threats to others. Anyone who saw him would think he was the actual bank manager and that my uncle was an impostor mistakenly sitting in the manager's office. The lame man was feared, and everyone, as I quickly learned, tried to gain his favour.

As we got into the car, not knowing where he would take me this time, he said:

'This country thrives on hypocrisy... If you're not like that, you won't succeed.'

He patted my shoulder gently, adding:

'I'm trying to teach you lessons that will benefit you in the future, kid.'

I smiled, without any conviction or agreement with his idea, without understanding why. It wasn't about whether he was right or wrong, but because, from a young age, I felt I should live a straight life, without being able to find the necessary logic for that or understanding whether a person can control their actions, paths in life, and behaviour.

It was too early for my uncle to return home, as I had learned from the limping man that they were closing the accounts for the year and planning the budget for the new year, which would keep my uncle at the bank until just before sunset. The car sped off at the usual insane speed, which I had started to get used to, and we didn't stop until about 15 minutes later in front of a place covered by a trellis near a side street behind the main road that runs alongside the country's main airport. I knew this because I could see planes parking on the ground in front of me. It was the first time I had ever seen a real plane up close. The limping man seemed to be watching me out of the corner of his eye and said:

'One day, you'll be travelling in one of those… don't think too much about it.'

We entered a tiny restaurant in a narrow alley, with a few customers eating sandwiches, some standing because the place was too small. Personally, I don't like eating sandwiches; I prefer to eat directly from a plate with my hands, as I was used to at home, where we would all fight over the meal as if in a war, and rarely did anyone get full.

There was a man in his mid-fifties, elegantly dressed with a well-trimmed white beard, sitting on a comfortable chair at the entrance of the place. He caught my attention with his reddish skin and cheerful smile, which would have been pleasant if I hadn't learned in less than two weeks not to trust the first smile. The man greeted the incoming customers.

The limping man and I ate shawarma sandwiches, which I tasted for the first time, and he told me that this man was from Turkey and owned the place, though few people knew about it. He said:

'People go to worse, more miserable restaurants and pay more... Here, the food is good, and the price is fair.'

He asked me:

'Do you have a shawarma place in your town?'

He wasn't really asking; he was mocking because he knew the answer. I felt ashamed of my hometown and answered:

'It's the first time I've tasted it...'

'Did you like it?'

'Oh yes... It's amazing.'

I wasn't lying; the shawarma sandwich was incredible, unlike anything I'd ever tasted before, probably because it was my first time.

The important thing was that I told the truth while listening from the man to the rest of his comments about the importance of taking care of money, saying that just as a person works hard to earn it, they should know how to use it wisely. He would bring money into almost every conversation. I noticed this about him but didn't pay much attention because it was his habit.

I saw him eat voraciously and order more sandwiches and refreshing juice cocktails. The man loved juices very much. He urged me to have more like him, but I refused because I was genuinely full; my stomach was just a small vessel.

After we finished and stood by the car under a neem tree, he lit a cigarette. He smoked occasionally but not often, and never in front of his master, the manager. He took a deep puff like someone seeking the unknown, and after a moment of silence, he said to me:

'I want to ask you something...'

'Go ahead, what do you want?'

'First... do you agree that we've become friends?'

I looked at him and smiled, which he took as agreement. He then said:

'We'll continue in the car... come on.'

I struggled to climb into the car; it was very high for my height. He started the engine but didn't drive forward; instead, he put a cassette he took from his pocket into the car's player, playing a popular song by a folk singer. He began to sway and dance before telling me:

'I'll give you whatever money you need, anything you ask for… but I have one request… listen to me carefully.'

I focused on what he was going to say, feeling a little uneasy. What could he want from me?

'You must not let your uncle know about your outings with me… do you understand that?'

'But I think he knows that I go out with you…'

'I mean, if he asks you where you've been, where we went… the point is, where we go, do you understand? If he confronts you with such a question, find another answer!'

'But maybe someone will tell him… maybe that will happen?'

'It won't happen… Do you think someone will spy on our steps? Why, are we committing a crime?… And who would do that… Do you mean… the old guard… or the bank guard… or… they know nothing about life, all of them… and the important thing is that none of them speaks, they're all under my command… cowards… Understand that… and you too must obey me, do you understand?'

The last sentences about obedience, he said jokingly… at least that's how it seemed to me.

I meant what I said. I wasn't naive despite my young age. Perhaps he would understand me… or not… I feared getting involved in explaining to him that what I meant by my question about who would tell my uncle was the great lady. She doesn't want me to stay in the house and may hate me because I come from people she doesn't like, her husband's relatives… and that's why she might spy on my steps or harass me… But I chose not to talk about it and kept it to myself. However, the limping man was much smarter than me, and he knew a lot about life and this family in particular... He was humming along with the folk singer and casting glances at me before he faced me and said:

'What did you mean, boy?'

Was he fooling me from the beginning and didn't notice my question, or was he trying to outsmart me... I didn't reply because I felt he wanted to say something... He continued:

'You mean the great lady... hahaha, she won't do anything to you... just stay under my protection... this house is under my control...'

My confusion increased... What did the man want from me? He had warned me against excessive trust in people and the dangers of this big city... Now he was playing the same role on me... Should I trust him or not... And he continued to read my thoughts as he had quickly come to understand my thinking, or so it seemed to me from my outings with him. He told me:

'Forget about all of them... Think about your future, boy, and stop thinking badly about anything... Be brave in facing circumstances and all possibilities, that's how you become a man... Tell me, why did you leave your father's house in the first place? Isn't it because life there is unbearable... I will make you live a happy life... Don't think of your uncle, or your aunt, or the red devil... No one offers you a service for free in this world... Do you understand this, boy... If your uncle is hosting you in his house or made you promises, know that it won't last long, not just because his wife is fierce... Do you know what this word means?... But also because your uncle, even if he seems like a good man who loves good, has a goal you don't see now. Boy, your uncle is no exception and never will be, especially with that woman made from the ashes of hell... But as I told you, don't be afraid of her at all...'

I was surprised at how he knew the details of my story and family when I hadn't told him about these things before! Moreover, he never asked me about them before! Also, how could he control the great lady? Does he have some secret connection with her? Should I ask him? It would be inappropriate; the man should say what he wants and at the right time. I began to feel that there was some hidden purpose behind his friendship that had not yet become clear to me. But the time was approaching… no rush. I heard him continue:

'You want to complete your education… you'll just be wasting your time then… You know how to read, write, and do math, that's enough… A person in this life only needs that…'

He pointed to his head and tapped it twice with his finger. He started the car and drove off at a crazy speed without finishing the story… What was the reason he was so keen on keeping my uncle unaware of our daily trips or where. What made him so insistent on keeping my uncle in the dark about our outings or where exactly we were going? This really troubled me. I was also preoccupied with trying to figure out what he truly wanted from me, why he was so generous with money. There was a mystery here, something I couldn't quite understand. I felt that I needed to keep this secret between us, not just because he had warned me, but also because my relationship with my uncle wasn't deep. Even though I lived in his house, he never really discussed personal matters with me or asked where I was going or where I had been.

He didn't quickly tell me what he wanted, and I waited for a second week. We continued going out together as usual. He would visit several companies in different buildings across the city, leaving me in the car. We went several times to the shawarma shop, where I saw the Turkish man with his charming smile, greeting his customers. I felt that the man was paying special attention to me. I caught him more than once stealing glances at me, as if he wanted to say that he had known me for a long time. He would glance at me, then look toward the opposite wall, then return to gaze at me from afar. I didn't pay much attention to it, nor did I dare to ask him about it.

As we were on the road, it crossed my mind to ask the limping man, and he replied:

'Don't worry too much. If there's something important, you'll find out one day.'

He said that with a half-smile, almost laughing. I wondered if he was hiding a secret or perhaps thinking about something particular. I had a feeling that his response had something to do with my question about the Turkish man's interest in me. I decided to stop worrying about it. We picked up some groceries for the house, went to the bank, and I sat in the room with the picture of the country's president. Life seemed the same—nothing new—as I waited to understand why the limping man was afraid that my uncle might find out about our daily outings.

During one of our daytime trips, he told me about his life. It seemed to me that some of the details were fabricated. He had a wild imagination, blending reality with fiction.

He briefly told me that he had a miserable childhood in a family similar to ours, except that his father died early, leaving him to face the cruel days washed in pain. His mother was patient and hardworking, doing whatever she could to bring happiness to her children, who eventually scattered across the earth. She sold everything in the market but gained nothing but regret. They left, not even bothering to contact her or inquire about her well-being, not even through a simple verbal message that could be sent by a villager.

He said one of his brothers is a senior official at the United Nations in New York, and as for him… he is the only one who sends money to his mother every month.

I might have dozed off and woken up, the lessons and stories never ending. We would have arrived home by then, and he would be unloading the groceries, chatting with the old guard and asking him why his son was late this time. I wouldn't hear what they said clearly, or I'd be too lost in my thoughts, my mind stirred by the limping man's stories, imagining that my mind might be kind and longing for those I fled from. But I decided there would be no going back—that was my wisdom, which I was determined to stick to.

Days passed without me knowing whether I was happy or not, until one day nearly disrupted the plan I had conceived since my escape, thinking of a new world. That day, we had returned, as usual, the limping man and I, and he took out two bottles of refreshing juice from the car. He started gulping his down while I sipped mine slowly.

We suddenly heard loud banging on the outer door, even though there was an electric bell that could be pressed to alert those inside the house. The guard hurried to open the gate, and a group of people—women, men, and children—rushed in. My mother was at the forefront, along with two of my brothers. I saw a large lorry parked outside, and four men from our neighbourhood were getting down a man from a bed, carrying him like a dead crocodile being dragged out of the river by hunters. It was my father.

My mother scolded me a lot, saying I ran away without informing her. She said:

'True, our home is unbearable with the misery your father brings, but look at him now—he can't speak or move.'

I looked at him. His eyes were closed, as if he had plunged into water and emerged. His tongue hung out, and tears flowed down his cheeks as he caught a glimpse of me in his stupor. He was conscious but exhausted. I couldn't hold back my tears as I hugged my mother and brothers, telling her:

'I had to do it... but I don't know why!'

The great lady had come out, cursing loudly. Her welcome was very hostile towards my family. I hated her immensely. My mother hurried to kiss her hand, an act that made my heart ache and intensified my curses on existence.

The curses ended as the old lady went inside and closed the small door leading to the inner part of the house, leaving everyone outside, shouting:

'Wait for this fool to come and solve your endless problems.'

My uncle arrived just before sunset. My father was groaning and fighting his pain. According to one of my brothers, he had overindulged in drink two days before. He spent the night in that distant house on the outskirts of town, where drunkards and prostitutes from West Africa gather. His excessive drinking had knocked him out, and he fought three men over one of those women, resulting in his current condition.

The story was strange to me because I knew my father drank, hit my mother, and stole car fuel, but I never knew him to be unfaithful to my mother. Yet, I had to believe this story.

My mother told me as we rode in my uncle's big car, with the limping man driving us to the city's main hospital:

'Your father couldn't handle your absence... he cried for two days... you are the reason for this.'

I didn't know whether to believe what was being said. Could it be true that he missed me and cried for me so much that he ended up chasing prostitutes and overdrinking in that wretched house on the town's outskirts?

My head was spinning with a mix of fear for the future, pity for my father, and a strong resolve that I would never return there—never.

They admitted my father to the intensive care unit. In our town, there isn't a modern hospital. Rather, there's one built during the English era, now ruins sheltered by the ghosts of the neighbouring cemetery.

I sat under a tree with my mother, brothers, and some men from the neighbourhood who had come to the hospital from the village. In our town, people will come to you even if you're their enemy if you are sick or have a death in the family. Despite my father's actions, he always made it a point to visit people on every occasion, even if he had to go drunk.

My mother took me aside, urging me to return with them once my father recovered. I promised her, but deep down, I wasn't convinced.

My uncle saved me from that decision. After my father recovered a week later, he told my mother and father:

'Let him stay with us. He'll be like our son. You know how lonely it is for me and my wife. Our daughter won't come back from India until the summer.'

My father, who had become as strong as a horse, replied:

'He can stay, but he must return as soon as your daughter comes back for her vacation. This is a man's promise to a man.'

He playfully shook my uncle's hand, although I knew he didn't like him. My mother was happy because this playful gesture held significant meaning for her.

During the week we spent in the hospital and until we returned to my uncle's house and my family left, the great lady had disappeared from the house. The limping man, who is the keeper of secrets here, told me she had quarrelled with my uncle and gone to her family's house on the city's outskirts. She would surely return once she knew the enemies had gone. He said to me:

'She does that a lot… she loves your uncle very much.'

The limping man laughed and took me in the evening through alleys and side streets until we reached a house in a slum area lacking lighting, with unpleasant smells, probably because it was close to a sewage disposal site.

We entered through the short door of the house. The great lady was there, sitting next to an elderly woman and a young man who looked like her, probably her brother, as he resembled her. He was bald and wearing a headset on his right ear, swaying to music.

For the first time, I saw the great lady's body; she was sitting in a short dress that barely reached her knees and had no sleeves. Her right breast was prominently pushed forward, very large. She looked like one of those prostitutes my father fought the three men over, as described in the story I heard. I used to see women like that in the town market during the day when they came to buy their night's supplies.

As soon as we arrived and greeted her mother, she stood up, hurriedly put on her toub dress, grabbed her bag, and, in my eyes, suddenly and without warning, transformed from a miserable creature sitting on the edge of the bed into a fierce being. Her brother didn't get up to greet us; he simply extended his smooth, soft hand, without looking at us, and continued to sway as he carried the small player outside to an alley behind the room that seemed to be the whole house. That room had walls covered with pictures of semi-naked women, probably movie or music stars, but I don't have much knowledge in that area.

I was astonished as I compared her lifestyle to her family's. I wanted to ask the limping man about it, but it wasn't the right time since the great lady was sitting in the front seat of the car next to him. She looked different with the contrast I had just discovered.

We stopped at an ice cream shop at her request. The limping man got out, bought three cones, and handed me one. She was licking hers in an odd manner, swirling her tongue over the top of the creamy white ice cream, which reminded me of the sheep back in the green island of our hometown as they licked the clover.

She didn't speak until we were close to the house. She glanced back at me as I sat crouched on the seat, smiled at me in a way that seemed strange and unexpected, and then winked with her left eye. For the first time, I was able to see her face in great detail—she had thick eyebrows, large eyes, full lips, and a pointed nose. I didn't understand the reason behind her sudden friendliness.

When we got out of the car, she asked me to carry her bag inside the house. The request seemed odd since the bag was small and didn't require assistance, but I complied. The limping man watched me with a smile, and I understood from his wink that I should follow orders.

This was my first time inside the inner part of the house, which, despite its modest exterior, appeared spacious, large, and well-organized inside. There were flowers everywhere, cool air, and paintings on the walls, including one of my uncle with the great lady on their wedding day in black and white, and another of my cousin, who I knew little about except that she had been studying computer science in India for two years. She looked stunning with her tall stature and long hair, dressed in a completely white suit. One of her legs was straight, the other bent, and her right hand was placed on her upper thigh. She resembled my uncle more in her outward appearance, though her facial features were closer to her mother's.

Shawarma

When the lady saw me staring at the picture, not paying attention as I put down her bag, she said:

'That's my daughter. Do you like her?'

I didn't comment, only returned a smile that she interpreted as admiration for my cousin, then I headed toward the outer door. Before I could grab the handle, I suddenly felt a strong hand gripping it and locking the door. It was the great lady, who grabbed me by the waist and lifted me—my weight was light—throwing me onto a thickly covered woolen couch. I was taken aback and puzzled by her behaviour. Was this well-mannered woman turning to such disgraceful conduct?

I despised her internally, but I lacked the strength to resist as she showered me with kisses, making strange moaning sounds I had never heard before. She said:

'You're handsome, boy. Don't you know that? Have you ever looked at your face in the mirror?'

I wasn't sure about this description, though some people had mentioned it before, especially some of the men in the neighbourhood who would chase after children and boys my age. Once, one of them chased me into an abandoned house nearby and tried to tear off my pants violently, but I fought back and eventually defeated him. I told my older brother, who took revenge by stabbing him in the rear with a knife, as he had done to my sister, as he was skilled in this method of retaliation.

I had defeated that man despite his strength, but this woman was incredibly strong, as if her hands were forged from the stones of mountains. Finally, she satisfied her desires with me. I had never experienced anything like being under the control of a female before, whether an older woman or a younger one. She moaned loudly while I was thinking about how to escape this situation.

Eventually, she let me go. She stood up, her dress had fallen to the floor, and she stared at me as if she was seeing me for the first time. It ended with her giving me a warning:

'Don't tell anyone.'

This incident left me terrified of the days ahead. If I were to stay here as my uncle promised, I didn't know what the coming nights would bring. I would have to be cautious. She originally didn't want me here. Now, if she wanted me to stay, I would be threatened if I didn't satisfy her suppressed desires. I was puzzled by the change in her attitude towards me. Had she not noticed me before? She used to pressure my uncle and insult me, calling me the scum of the earth.

Over time, people can decipher some of the world's mysteries without having to exhaust their minds with futile persistence; at the right moment, every puzzle solves itself. This is what became clear to me later.

That night, I was scared, alone in the room. I left the inner part of the house terrified, finding that the limping man had left. The guard had gone to spend time with some of the old men who gathered under a streetlight, reminiscing about their past experiences. My uncle hadn't returned yet, which was unusual. I saw the lady's ghostly figure moving around in the inner courtyard in her nightgown, but she didn't approach my room.

Later, I saw my uncle arrive in the car with a sheep in the trunk. The guard entered with him and quickly carried the sheep into a small pen near my room. The bleating of the sheep echoed in my mind, interrupting the dread I felt from the great woman's earlier attack.

I considered telling the limping man the next day when we went out together, as usual, but I decided to keep this secret to myself. Revealing it might lead to undesirable consequences.

Eventually, I fell into a deep sleep after an exhausting day, and I didn't dream of anything. I only woke up early to perform the dawn prayer at the mosque, where the old guard stood beside me. On the way back from prayer, he informed me that my uncle was preparing for a party he would host at the house tomorrow for some high-ranking people. He said this happens once or twice a year.

In the morning, the limping man was late. He didn't arrive until noon, carrying many supplies along with two more sheep. The young cook was busy with hard work in the kitchen. The old guard slaughtered the three sheep, and we helped him with the skinning and meat cutting. The cook then began his arduous task.

In the afternoon, the limping man arranged the outer garden. A small truck delivered a set of tables and chairs, which were neatly arranged by skilled workers who didn't appear to be Sudanese. I asked the limping man and he told me:

'They are from neighbouring Ethiopia. Thousands of them work in companies and homes. They have entire neighbourhoods in the capital.'

By nightfall, the site was ready. The bright lights, the cushioned chairs, the tables covered with rainbow-patterned sheets.

Two Ethiopian girls from the same company arrived to help with the arrangement and serve drinks to the guests who started arriving one after another. So, these were the high-ranking people the old guard had mentioned. They wore a mix of traditional attire—jalabiyas and turbans—and Western-style suits with ties. Among them were three women. Strangely, the great lady didn't appear among them; the limping man had taken her out in the car.

I saw everyone sitting around the tables. I was standing off to the side, helping with various tasks as requested. My uncle, dressed in an elegant blue suit and holding his pipe, appeared more youthful than usual. There was a lady joking with him, but he seemed not to pay much attention to her.

My uncle stood before everyone. There was a microphone connected to some speakers. He began speaking. I didn't understand much of what he said, or perhaps I wasn't paying much attention.

He was telling them about that so-called party and how we needed to increase our efforts in the coming phase. He spoke of complex challenges that needed to be overcome, the importance of involving women in higher structures, and the war that was ravaging the country and depleting budgets. For the first time, I heard about this war. In our northern town, no one had mentioned it before.

Another man, who was fully obese, spoke about charitable projects for orphans, the elderly, widows, and homeless children affected by the war. He was followed by a lady who recited a poem, of which I don't remember much, except that she repeatedly said, 'O precious homeland.' For about two hours, everyone spoke. The applause was frequent.

The two Ethiopian women were distributing drinks. This time, they distributed bottles that looked unusual to me; they were not the canned or bottled juices I knew. From a distance, I read the label, which said 'Scotch whisky'. It was a strange drink to me; they poured a little of it, just like the local wine, into long, transparent glasses. Within half an hour, everyone was quite disoriented; they were like drunkards or were indeed drunk.

I learned from the limping man, who had returned after dropping off the great lady at her mother's house, when I asked him, curious about what was happening:

'This drink is called whisky. It's a type of alcohol but imported, unlike the kind they make from dates in your town.'

He laughed loudly, his laughter piercing through the drunkards' jokes, and their prepared to tell a string of lewd jokes. I heard some of them with amusement and others with irritation, while the three ladies joined in the laughter and told jokes as they swayed their necks towards the men. Their head coverings had fallen off, revealing their hair.

Finally, dinner was served, and everyone devoured it with excessive greed. I watched the scene before me, remembering what they had said earlier about the famine in the western part of the country, and what someone else had read from a paper, mentioning specific figures, about infants dying because their mothers couldn't provide them with milk.

The limping man and I sat in a corner eating together. He had brought one of those bottles with him and had hidden a box with more bottles under the bed in my room. He sipped the whisky with his eyes closed every time he took a gulp. After a few minutes, he sat on the floor to continue eating and drinking. I asked him:

'Which party are they talking about, and why are they here?'

He looked at me as if to signal that it was not the right time for questions, but he answered slowly and laboriously:

'They are the decision-makers in this country. They are the ones who control your fate and mine.'

He laughed again, his laughter cutting through the noise of the drunken guests who were engrossed in their meal. Eventually, the large gate opened, and the huge cars departed with their owners, who hopped into them with surprising agility despite their lazy walking till they reached the cars.

I saw the lady who had been clinging to my uncle from early on was still trying to joke with him, but he seemed uninterested. After that they all left while the limping man stayed with me that night in the room, emptying one bottle after another from the box. I slept on the floor on a plastic mattress, while he sprawled on the bed's blanket, snoring loudly and passing gas, sometimes mocking and talking to himself as if he were awake. I feared that the night would not end safely.

When I woke up early in the morning, as usual, for the dawn prayer at the mosque, I found that the limping man had already risen before dawn and left, as if he were no longer the tired and exhausted person, he appeared to be just hours before.

He came back at eight in the morning to take me with him on our daily errands. On this particular day, he gave me a bundle of money. It was a large amount for me—not as much as the old man's money that the senior officer had stolen—but it was the largest sum I had ever received in my life. He said to me:

'Today, you will start working with me. Agreed?'

I had no idea about the nature of the work he had previously mentioned, and he had been careful not to let anyone else know about it. We would go to a specific building, and instead of me being in the car, he would take my place behind the wheel. Meanwhile, I would climb up dilapidated and newly-built buildings, often using dimly lit staircases due to power outages, and rarely using elevators, most of which were out of order in the city. The elevators were also frightening to me. I would carry small envelopes and distribute them to specific individuals. Client number such-and-such on such-and-such floor... wearing jeans and having curly hair. Client number such-and-such on the ground floor without hands... disabled. Place the envelope on his lap and come back. Be careful not to be seen. These were the instructions.

Days passed as I performed my work with complete accuracy, without having the right to ask about the contents of the envelopes. I could feel that they were not solid; they were soft, almost too soft. If I had run my long, dirty nails over them, I could have torn the envelope and seen what was inside. But I didn't do that because I had to adhere strictly to what was entrusted to me. I liked to perform my job well. The clients would receive the envelopes without offering thanks or any expressions of gratitude. They mostly looked intimidating, with no signs of affection, smiles, or friendly gestures, as if they were from another world.

After several days, the same client gave me an envelope in exchange for my envelope. It didn't take much intelligence to know what was in the envelope I received; it was stuffed with cash. A fortune we amassed in half a day.

The limping man was delighted as he drove the car at breakneck speed before we went, as usual, to the shawarma shop at least once or twice a week. There, the Turkish man with the lovely smile, who had come to know me well and showed increased interest in me, would greet me by shaking my hands firmly, patting my shoulder gently, and saying, 'Good luck, young man.'

The limping man didn't need to ask me if anyone knew about the work I was doing with him. He had trusted me completely and recognised my worth. He once said to me:

'I trust you more than I trust myself. You have a bright future, believe me, because you understand responsibility. One day, you will become something great in this country.'

His promises to me and his instilling of hope made me feel important and that one day I would have value in this country, just as he expected for me.

Ever since I fled on the train and the months that have passed, I've been wondering how tomorrow will be for me. I must succeed in the end, otherwise, my decision that day would have been wrong. I don't want to torture myself with the thought that my judgment was inaccurate in the past.

The limping man had been a motivator for me, and with him, I became independent in earning money. Within weeks, my small savings box hidden in my room was filled with new banknotes from my work, and I didn't know what to spend it on. I thought of sending some to my mother, but I knew she would immediately hand it over to my father, who would spend it on his drinking and my mother's humiliation. I decided not to do that.

I continued to be dedicated to my work, which I had gotten used to, until one morning when I went out as usual to wait for the limping man at the street corner, where he no longer came directly to the house in recent days without explaining why.

My uncle had spotted me; for some reason, he had returned from the bank even though he had left the house early, where he had been taken by the limping man as he did daily.

His face was different that morning; he was not the uncle I had known in recent months. If he didn't speak, he at least didn't show any positive or negative emotions. He stopped the car next to me, driving it alone while holding the steering wheel with one hand and his pipe with the other.

I expected the limping man to be inside when the car stopped and hurried towards it, only to find my uncle shouting at me angrily:

'Come on... Get in...'

I got in. He didn't speak to me and seemed angry. He drove the car recklessly, just like the limping man did. I didn't understand what was happening until he stopped at one of the buildings I was familiar with, one of those I visited daily with the envelope and carried the money.

The old man who was sitting near the building's entrance was seated in his torn plastic chair. He greeted my uncle

while ignoring me as if he didn't know me. I didn't understand what was happening until the old man spoke:
'He himself... he is the one who works with him,'
My uncle asked me directly:
'What are you doing with the limping man?'
I wasn't nervous. I was just doing my job and receiving my salary. I told him that I used to distribute envelopes at the limping man's request, which happened daily except on weekends, and that the man in front of me was one of my clients, even if he ignored me. My uncle said:
'Alright... Come on.'
The old man looked at me strangely, as if he expected me to say something other than the truth. I felt this, and heard my uncle mumbling:
'I know who is responsible... I know him well.'
We got back in the car and returned home. The limping man was waiting for us, terrified, in front of the door while the old guard was hiding behind his external room near the door, waiting to understand what was happening.
The weather was clearly tense. Something strange was going on. The great woman was shouting loudly inside the house, and I couldn't distinguish what she was saying.
My uncle slapped the limping man hard, multiple times. The man bent down to kiss my uncle's feet, who looked completely different that day, confirming to me that with each passing hour.
We all went inside the inner part of the house. The woman was in her underwear, continuing to scream, her hair dishevelled, and she wailed hysterically.
The limping man pointed to her behind my uncle, mumbling:
'She is the reason for this... She wants the money.'
My uncle asked the limping man:
'Why didn't you tell me from the beginning?'

'I couldn't, sir... You know I can't refuse the lady's request.'

My uncle asked us to leave, and we both went outside while he stayed inside with his wife.

After a few minutes, the situation calmed down. The woman's cries faded, replaced by laughter. I saw the excitement in the limping man's eyes as he slapped my shoulder hard, saying:

'I knew it was that damned old man who did this.'

'Which old man! What's wrong with what we're doing?'

He didn't answer me, and I understood that there was something wrong with the work we were doing. After a while, my uncle took me to the guard's room, sat me on the floor, and sat next to me. He spoke to me calmly, having returned to his usual self:

'Did you know what you were doing?'

'I don't know. I was helping with the work.'

He pointed at me with his forefinger, warning me gently:

'You are still young. In any case, what you were doing could have led you to prison. Don't repeat it. Consult me on any step you want to take.'

I promised my uncle to comply. He only asked me to inform him of my steps. I thought he would stop me from going out with the limping man, but he didn't mention it.

For the rest of the day, the limping man was absent. In the evening, the woman was alone, and the old guard had gone for the evening prayer. She called me to enter the inner part of the house. I entered; I had no choice but to comply. She performed the same act with me as before. I was embarrassed, while she showed no shame. She sang and danced with her legs and large breasts visible through her transparent dress. she turned off the large stereo next to the window. She said to me:

'Don't worry about what your uncle says. Tomorrow, you will go with the limping man as usual'

I was silent. What could I say? I didn't think much about it. I said:

'But my uncle warned me.'

I was scared. Suddenly, I felt a shiver and realised that this house was a huge deception for me. I heard her laughing as she restarted the music and resumed dancing, shaking her large hips towards me:

'Your uncle... Hahaha... Oh boy, don't be so naive. This kingdom, I am its mistress. Do you understand?'

I didn't need to be smart to understand what she was saying. It was clear from the first days I arrived that the lady was everything here. She was the one in charge, and my uncle was just a toy in her hands. She controlled him, the old guard, and the limping man, who did whatever she wanted and knew her secrets. He feared her more than he feared my uncle. I understood this better the following noon when the limping man took me under the lady's pressure, who said to me:

'If you don't take him and do your job as usual, you won't stay in this house'

I no longer wanted to stay here. I was now in an incomprehensible situation, doing something wrong that I didn't fully understand!

I got in the car with the limping man. He turned on the stereo and danced a lot, just like his lady. He had a strange smell that day, just like the lady's when she attacked me, an incomprehensible smell that made a person crazy, reckless, and sometimes kind.

The limping man laughed exaggeratedly and without reason. He drove the car at an incredible speed. I was afraid of the speed and his actions. He said to me:

'A coward won't do anything for his future, boy. Don't be afraid.'

Then he fell silent for a moment as if he was looking at a distant point in space, the empty street, which was crowded with cars he was skilfully overtaking, said:

'She knows everything... She is the great lady here... Don't be afraid... Your uncle won't do anything... I'm telling you this because I know you're very scared since yesterday.'

'That's true. I'm scared, but I don't understand what's happening to me or around me!'

He laughed a lot. He said:

'It doesn't matter if we know everything around us... That's the rule of life. Do you understand?'

He sped up to a fast street, moving away from the city a little to the south. He increased the speed of the car and spoke to himself, 'I will take my revenge on that old man.' I assumed he was referring to the one who my uncle had taken me with him to him and pointed at me as the limping man's assistant.

I wanted to ask him about what had happened, but the sound of the car engine, with the window next to him open, left no chance for anyone to hear the other, with the noise of trucks stopping at the checkpoints.

My uncle's large car sped along and no one from the police stopped it. The limping man would wave to them, and they would exchange greetings with smiles and sometimes the blowing of whistles they carried.

The speed had increased too much, and we were approaching a large truck. We were so close it felt like we would collide. The truck seemed to be right in front of us when I lost track of what happened.

It felt like I was in a dream when I woke up in a place I immediately recognised as the same hospital where my father had spent days after being brought from those clashes in the village. Nurses in white were around me. They informed me that I had undergone surgery on my foot and that I would suffer walking straight from now on after the accident we had. I wanted to know the fate of the limping man. Where was he? He wasn't in the room where I was lying. There was another bed here, but no one was in it. I asked them:

'Where is he?'

They knew who I meant. They were looking at each other without explaining to me what had happened. They remained silent until my uncle arrived an hour later. He greeted me kindly and told me that I had miraculously survived certain death. His face showed a deep affection for me, for some reason I couldn't interpret or know if I was imagining it or if it was real.

I looked at him as the smoke from his pipe rose in the emptiness of the room, while I struggled to recall those moments that seemed almost imaginary. When the car was lifted high into the air, then hit us far away on the edge of the street. The limping man had screamed loudly, groaning. After that, I remembered nothing.

My uncle said to me:

'You will be discharged from the hospital today... We didn't tell your family so they wouldn't worry.'

I asked him:

'Where is he?'

He looked at me. He knew that a close bond had formed between us in the past few months, even if it seemed suspicious or shrouded in mystery to him. What mattered was that it was deep and intimate. I could almost see him saying that through his facial expressions before he ignored my question and repeated:

'You will be discharged in an hour.'

I understood; the matter was clear. My friend and the man who cared for me had passed away. It was that thing they call death. The experience of the limping man's departure was harsh for me. He was one of the few people who cared for me in my youth, making me feel valued as a human being with potential and a future, unlike my home, where the windows of hope were always shut.

I couldn't believe it; it took me a long time to come to terms with it, but eventually, I did. Before that happened, other events had taken place in my uncle's house, leading to my second escape. I decided to leave that cursed house!

Limpness became a defining characteristic of mine, a distinctive feature. I walked with half a foot on the ground while the other struck hard, but I didn't need to use a crutch. My limp was somewhat similar to that of my friend. Sometimes, I felt pain from this disability that befell me in my youth, but I remembered it was God's will, and I had to obey it. Over time, I got used to my new appearance and gait, and I no longer thought about it.

I had imagined that the house would be filled with sorrow over the limping man's departure, but that did not happen as I expected. No one seemed to care except for my uncle, who appeared sad for two days after I was discharged from the hospital, then returned to his usual self. As for the great lady, I didn't know if she was sad or not. She continued her usual routines, going out in the evening with my uncle, staying out late at night. She bought new sets of clothes and shoes that she changed daily. She even changed almost all the furniture in the house. I knew preparations were underway to welcome my cousin, who would arrive in a few days to spend her school break.

I didn't go out much during the day as I used to. I started spending my days at home, responding to the lady's calls from time to time, following her orders to do this and that:

organize this thing, clean the window glass, wash the dishes in the inner kitchen, wipe the furniture, clean the bathroom. In short, I had become her servant. My uncle saw this but did not intervene. Strangely, she no longer behaved inappropriately with me. She seemed balanced, serious, and sometimes frightening, and mostly modest. I saw her more than once performing her prayers on time in her room.

During those days, the smell I used to sense in her moments of madness disappeared. I told myself perhaps the limping man's death affected her and made her change her behaviour. Some people fear death when it takes someone they know closely.

She would call me from time to time. 'Hey, limping one, come here…'

It was painful, but I had to accept it; there was no room for objection. I felt uncomfortable, like the place no longer suited me, but I had no choice but to be patient, as my uncle had promised me that school would start soon, and he would send me back to school. This would solve half of my problem with this lady, especially since the problem was mainly during the day when I would be at school, and at night she had other things to occupy her away from me.

Days passed before the schools opened and before my cousin arrived, for whom the whole house was preparing.

One day, I entered my room to find that the piggy bank where I kept my earnings from my outings with the limping man had been stolen. It was still in its place under the bed but emptied, with its lock broken.

Who did this? Who stole my hard-earned money? I didn't need much time to figure it out. As soon as I headed to the main courtyard of the house, near the fountain, where the parrot was mimicking my new walk, I spotted a tall, bald young man emerging from the old guard's room and approaching me. He quickly twisted my arm with force, without any introduction, before saying to me:

'You insolent one, you won't sleep in my room tonight. Do you understand?'

I immediately knew it was the guard's son, who had just returned from his trip. He was in his twenties, obnoxious, self-deluded, ugly in appearance, thinking he was smart. Many qualities I attributed to him from the first moment.

He didn't let go of me, still holding my hand and twisting it until it was about to break before his father, who was watching from a distance, ignored it.

He was rude, as it seemed. Finally, he let go of me, throwing me back with force, repeating his threat that I should leave the room, followed by saying:

'I took the price for letting you stay in my room all this time.'

He showed me a wad of money he pulled from the pocket of his long trousers. He was challenging me brazenly, and I had no way to resist him. Who could I complain to? I decided to tell my uncle about it that evening, and he responded calmly, seemingly indifferent:

'You can share the room together... What's the problem?'

He called him, and the obnoxious one came. My uncle told him the decision. He appeared obedient in front of him. But as soon as my uncle and his wife left that evening for their usual shopping trips for their daughter, the guard's son started provoking me again. He hit me with a thick stick he brought from his father's room, and the father participated in the crime, watching without being able to comment or speak.

The son didn't care whether his father was there or not. A large part of my back was bruised and bleeding. I found myself in a difficult situation that was unbearable. I had no hope other than to leave this house. This uncle seems to have no power to help or harm me.

When my uncle and the great lady returned, parked the car inside the house and the guard's son helped them carry the stuff inside. A bunch of bags filled with what… God knows!

He acted with them as if nothing had happened, while I remained lying on the ground in a dark corner of the courtyard, seeing nothing but my pain and tragedy. It seems the old lady noticed me, but she didn't speak to me.

After hours, everyone had gone to sleep. The lights inside the house were off, and a faint light was coming from the guard's room. The guard's son had returned from outside, staggering, seemingly drunk, and headed to the room he had taken over since the afternoon, throwing out my belongings. I had no place to lie down but in a corner of the courtyard, waiting for a miracle.

After a few minutes, I saw him jump from one of the internal house windows into one of the rooms. There wasn't enough light to see what happened next.

Curiosity overwhelmed me, wanting to understand what was happening. So, I listened closely by the window. The situation didn't require much to understand what was going on inside. Through the window, which wasn't securely closed, I clearly saw the rest of the scene that shocked me. The great lady was completely naked, lying on the carpet next to a woollen sofa, while the guard's son was lying on top of her.

This scene reminded me of my father in the village, who used to do such things without regard for time or respect for us. My mother had no choice but to submit to his tyranny. But was the guard's son imposing tyranny on the lady? It didn't seem that way. The situation appeared entirely intimate, and I heard her say to him:

'That idiot should have died; he saved us time, didn't he?'

With muffled laughter to avoid being caught, he asked her:

'I think you're behind what happened?!'

She laughed back, quietly, and I didn't hear her respond. In a broken voice that carried with the slight breeze starting to blow outside, I heard the obnoxious one reply:

'I'll get my driving license soon; one of the officers promised me that. And we'll continue the work... I know all the clients from my previous trips with the limping man.'

Then he asked her:

'Do you think this boy could be useful to us... What do you think?'

She screamed at him:

'No, I don't want him because his uncle found out he was working with the limping man.'

'So what's the point of him staying here?'

'His uncle wants him... He wants to send him back to school.'

'And do you want him?'

I heard her say:

'Now that you've come back to me, I don't want him anymore... hahaha... He doesn't know anything about life yet, and he's useless.'

She continued laughing in an inappropriate manner. I had to leave the window after I sensed that the guard's son got up and approached her. I saw him naked as well. The situation was clear before me—unbelievable. Does my uncle know about this? Is he asleep or awake? What kind of hell is this? I wondered in shock at what was happening before me.

I didn't think for long as I rushed back to where I used to sleep in the corner under the neem tree. I was exhausted, and in my sleep, I had many frightening nightmares. Once, I saw the limping man standing before me, threatening me with a knife. Then it was my father, and then the guard's son holding the knife, pointing it at my chest. My uncle was laughing a lot, and the great woman was watching, naked, while guzzling a bottle of imported alcohol, which was the star of that night's party.

When I woke up at dawn with the call to prayer, my life seemed like a dream. A headache surrounded me and troubled my soul. I headed to the mosque for prayer and then returned. The guard was walking beside me, not speaking, and I didn't feel like talking to him either—I had started to hate him after his recent actions.

I saw my uncle sitting and reading as usual, smoking his pipe. In the distance, the guard's son was sleeping in my bed in the room from which I had been kicked out. The place no longer suited me, but what could I do? Returning to the village was an impossibility—I would not go back. I remembered some of the limping man's advice: that a person creates their own destiny. So, I decided that morning, I would create my own destiny, and I acted on it.

That day, when I left the village, I didn't need anyone to inspire me to know that I was doing the right thing. The same scene would repeat itself today—I wouldn't need that someone, even if he was a man I learned from, who has now gone to the grave he dug for himself.

I seriously thought about the limping man from another perspective—was he doing good or evil? I didn't have an answer. But what troubled me was what I overheard in the conversation between the great lady and the guard's son, as she responded to his question about the man's fate with laughter.

Does this mean that she arranged for his death? Or at least set the stage for him to lose control that day, leading to his breakdown and death? Was she the one who exposed the fact that I was working with the limping man? Does my uncle know what the limping man was really up to?

I had no answers. I thought that the only thing worth exhausting my mind over was only finding my own salvation.

With the new morning, I had fled on my second journey!

Before I left, my uncle appeared to me in his rocking chair, like an old ghost in the nights of the village. I passed by the parrot to bid it farewell, but found it sleeping. I walked backward, my eyes fixed on the house that had sheltered me for several months.

3
Life in the street

The new city reveals a different face each time, one unlike the familiar scenes I had seen while driving around with the limping man. Now, I witness a world of contradictions and wonders—the remarkable and astonishing, as well as the things that make a person feel stifled and filled with contempt.

Perhaps this was a reflection of my emotions rather than a precise general thought. I was walking down a long street that started from my uncle's house—specifically from the main street adjacent to the house—and extended to a bridge connecting two cities. In reality, the large city consists of three cities connected by iron and concrete bridges spanning the rivers that flow from south to north. The old ones were built during the British years, and the second after they left the country.

Before I reached the end of the very long street at the bridge, I stopped. Security forces and police were closing off the area, preventing pedestrians and cars from passing. They were talking about the President of the Republic crossing through soon, which was why they were halting movement for him.

An hour, maybe more, passed before the motorcade arrived, led by speeding motorcycles, followed by long black cars and then other vehicles. They passed in front of me so fast that it was impossible to distinguish them. Compared to them, the limping man was slow in his driving, but it was God's will that took him to the heavens.

I continued walking, not knowing my destination, and considered returning to my uncle's house before dismissing the idea entirely. I didn't come here to be humiliated. I left my father's house because I couldn't accept injustice, and I wouldn't accept it here either. These people don't want me, and I won't stay with them for that reason. Perhaps if the limping man were still alive, things would be different.

I was, as usual, hungry and thirsty. I stopped at an ice cream vendor, used some of the money I had, and sipped a cup of homemade hibiscus juice. It tasted wonderful and more delicious than the imported juices my uncle gets from abroad with special recipes, along with that intoxicating drink.

From afar, I spotted an old man walking with a cane. I immediately recognised him as the companion I had left or who had left me at the train station. Thank God the bag is with me; I'm holding it in my left hand. I didn't let go of it and won't forget it—it's a trust, even if the money is stolen from it.

I turned into the adjacent street, which was almost an alley but bustling with people in a crowded area of the northern city among the three. Here, there was a bus station for local transport, a police station, a prison administration, and a cultural center for teaching singing. I was reading the signs in a flash as I tried to catch up with the old man. But he had disappeared into the second street on the right.

I hurried to catch up with him, but before I could reach him, fast-moving cars appeared in front of me, forcing me to wait for them to pass. I waited, and as a result, I lost sight of the man. It seemed to me as if he had boarded a bus that had stopped on the right, quickly leaving.

Could I still catch up with him? But I wasn't sure of his destination—perhaps he had entered the second corner of the small street or one of the many shops.

I spent nearly an hour moving between the streets without seeing him again, doubting whether I had really seen him the first time or just imagined it. I thought to myself that maybe if I had found him, he would have been my saviour—I do not know why I was overwhelmed with this feeling, even though it no longer mattered after I lost the old man, who, despite his cane, was able to walk quickly. I don't think he carried the cane to help him walk; he carried it out of habit, like many others do.

I continued walking again, crossing the bridge, watching the river on both banks. It seemed as if it was as anxious as I was about its future, quietly frothing, unlike how it is during the season of floods and high waters in the village.

My mind drifted back to my early years when I secretly learned to swim, as my mother forbade us from going to the river for fear of drowning. Suddenly, a thought came to me—I don't know exactly where it came from—as I looked toward the river. The image of the old man with the bag appeared in my mind, gesturing for me to keep moving forward and not to stop. He told me that my feet would lead me to where my destiny and salvation would be.

I walked for a long time until I was tired and exhausted. After an hour, I could no longer continue, and hunger overtook me. I found myself lying by the roadside next to a mosque in the city center. I wasn't alone—there were dozens, maybe hundreds, like me—people of all kinds and ages, with different faces and stories. It seemed that each one had a story behind them, and it seemed that I would become part of these many stories. Their conditions were miserable, and one look was enough to know that they had either come from the hell of the war said to be in the south of the country or from the famine in the west, or like me, from the east and north, having lost connection with their families.

I didn't wake up until I heard the sound of a large police car and the cries of passersby and others like me, the lost ones. The soldiers, dressed in blue, were mercilessly beating the street dwellers behind the mosque, picking up the elderly and children, throwing them into the car.

Behind it, you could hear the wails of infants and elderly women. The scene seemed like something out of the nightmares from the previous night, but it was real.

This was my country. This was the other face of the big city. Behind the banks, the colourful curtains, and the grand mansions, there was another face here—one of sorrow, tears, and crying. And I found myself thrown into the car like the others. One of them had grabbed me around the middle and flung me away like a lightweight ball, settling me in my spot among piles of foul-smelling bodies.

Inside the vehicle, it was dark, it was covered with iron from all sides except for a small door through which I had passed on my way in. The officer closed it tightly, the sounds of cursing and profanity ebbing and flowing like the waves of the river.

I don't know how long the prison car drove or how many streets and alleys it crossed before we arrived at a courtyard with high walls. They dragged us out like livestock. The soldiers were pulling us one by one, brutally, without any regard for age or decency, lining us up against the wall in a straight line.

There were already dozens who had arrived before us, in the same position. I heard an officer hurling insults, while another repeatedly stomped his boot on the ground, spewing racist slurs. 'You black! You slave!' Then he stopped in front of me, asking:

'What brought you here among this scum?'

I didn't respond to him; I just looked at him. He was so tall that it was difficult to observe him entirely. I focused on his face, which was scarred with clear vertical marks on his forehead as if cut by a sharp blade.

I heard him repeat the question before he grabbed me and threw me into the middle of the courtyard, then did the same to others.

The wailing of children and infants grew louder, the snoring of the elderly echoed around, and the curses never ceased. Then, they brought a large bowl of food—I couldn't tell what it was. Everyone scrambled for it like starving chickens, and I managed to secure a couple of bites, thanks to an elderly man who skilfully reached the bowl and handed me a portion of what he had caught.

I did not know how long we would remain here or why we were here either. No one to answer you. I spent the night in this prison where we could see the stars in a dark black sky. I did not sleep well; nightmares still haunted me, with images of my family, my uncle, the old man, the limping man, and the old guard's son in that strange position.

I suddenly woke up to the sound of the dawn call to prayer, where they stopped us in rows for prayer without paying attention to ablution. An elderly man with a long white beard led us in the prayer, ending it with a prayer to God to destroy the enemies of the faith and to support the mujahideen in the south of the country.

Three days passed in this way—nothing of value. Time passed by watching and studying the faces of the people around me, distracting myself with their quarrels and disputes, some of which I didn't understand as they were in languages I'd never heard before, likely local dialects. It was easy for one of them to scratch another with his long nails or stomp on his stomach.

I preferred to stay in a corner, fearing I might get hurt. This doesn't mean I wasn't harassed, but I didn't escape the beatings either. The guards watched without intervening, enjoying the fights as they smoked hookahs, patted their bellies, and laughed loudly before bringing us that large bowl of strange food that everyone would devour within minutes.

On the evening of the fourth day, one of the guards called me by name. I didn't know how he knew it, as they hadn't taken down any names. I doubt most of the people here even remember their names; their hardships in life probably leave them with little memory of anything but surviving the moment. I stood before a senior officer—another senior officer after the one at the train station who had stolen the old man's money.

The officer, a first lieutenant, said to me:

'Someone is here for you… He'll be here soon. He's concerned about you and wants to get you out of here.'

I had known military ranks since childhood because our house was near a police station. I said:

'But no one knows I'm here.'

'He's an important person anyway, and he asked for your release.'

My mind became preoccupied as I tried to figure out who could have seen me being thrown into the vehicle or entering this prison. Could it be my uncle who found out and came for me? But my uncle usually doesn't show much concern.

I didn't dwell too long on trying to find the answer because the old man with the bag was standing in front of me. I saw him, and tears welled up in my eyes. What brought him here? How did he know about me? My God, this fate is astonishing… how beautiful it is.

The man didn't speak much or reveal his identity to me, but I noticed how the officers treated him with great respect. It raised questions in my mind—how could an old, miserable man who travels by train suddenly become, as the officer said, 'important' in any way? It felt like a dream, as if he was playing a role in a theatrical act amusing to boys like me.

The man took me out of the prison to the neighbouring street, which was crowded with people. He thanked me repeatedly for taking care of his bag, without even knowing if the money was still inside or not. I tried to tell him, but he didn't listen. He smoked his cheap cigarette before we stopped in front of a refreshment stand. He ordered two cups of hibiscus juice, paid for them, handed one to me, and placed the other on the high table. We were standing.

He asked the shop owner if there was a toilet in the shop, and the owner pointed to a small wooden door at the back.

The old man excused himself to use the restroom. Minutes passed; I had finished my hibiscus juice. The man hadn't returned; he'd been in the toilet for a long time. The shop owner noticed and asked:

'Where is your companion? It seems he's taking a too long time.'

'Indeed, he has been in there for quite a while. I don't have a watch, but I think it's been half an hour.'

The shop owner said:

'Check by pushing the door. See if he's still in there.'

I went to the door and pushed it open; it wasn't locked. I pushed it inward, and it creaked, but the man wasn't there. No one was inside. Where did the old man disappear to this time? I don't think my eyes left the bathroom door. My head spun with confusion, and the man hadn't taken his bag or revealed his secret to me.

I returned to tell the shop owner, but he didn't seem too concerned. He said:

'Maybe he had something urgent and left in a hurry. He'll come back for you.'

I stayed by the shop, sitting on the ground, holding the same bag with the Qur'an and the prayer beads inside. There was nothing else to do but count the time, waiting for the old man to return or come out of an empty toilet. Several people had gone in and out of the restroom, including the shop owner. I myself went twice. The evening had grown late, midnight had passed, and the streets were gradually emptying of people. Public transport vehicles and minibuses became scarce on the main street. The lights dimmed, except for the streetlights where the scattered yellow light merged with the particles of the broken asphalt, washed by sewage water.

Once again, I found myself facing the deep question: what should I do, and how will I face the upcoming moments of life? Should I return to my uncle's house, where I thought he had come to get me out of prison, only to find that wasn't the case?

Finally, I placed my trust in God and nestled into a corner of the street next to the refreshment shop, where some people had already begun to sleep. In this city, almost any place can be a bed or a room. Along the night and the street, it seemed to me there was another version of those who were thrown into the police vehicle that day—old men, children, women, and I was part of them.

I threw myself into this fate and slept, exhausted. It was a risk that might send me back to prison, and the old man might not return to rescue me again. I didn't wake up until the dawn call to prayer, as usual. I hurried to a nearby mosque and prayed Fajr.

The mosque was large, and there were many rows of worshippers. Most of the street dwellers had come to pray, and I saw a boy about my age who had been sleeping next to me standing in the row ahead of me, yawning frequently, as if he hadn't completed his sleep.

The boy and I talked; he told me he had come from the south of the country after losing his family due to the war. He didn't know exactly where they were now, whether they were alive or dead—he wasn't sure.

Shortly after, as we stood at the street corner, a girl older than us appeared, that was clear from her tall stature, prominent breasts, and long braided hair. She had a distinct dark complexion. I felt a bit of admiration for her at first sight. She greeted my companion and glanced at me out of the corner of her eye without greeting me. She asked the boy:

'Where did this one come from?'

'He prayed with us in the mosque. I don't know. Ask him about his story.'

It seemed my presence with the boy didn't please her, as she gestured for me to move away. Unlike the other street children, she appeared neat, well-groomed, and attractive, with a distinctive scent of perfume. I felt a desire to know her secret, but she didn't give me the chance. She simply renewed her gesture for me to leave. Not being one to chase after others, I left and went my way, while she and the boy went together.

I was unsure what to do until I came up with a simple idea to save enough for food, just to get through today and tomorrow. I trusted myself and knew I would do something for my future. The words of the limping man echoed in my mind—how perseverance and patience were crucial. I decided not to let time defeat me and return to my old life. It was a stubbornness that was hard to understand, but it defined me.

The idea was to accompany one of those boys I had met earlier in the morning, who carried a small wooden box with a shoe-shining kit. I agreed to help him with his work in exchange for splitting the money, and sometimes I would carry the box instead of him while he rested.

I no longer knew peace or calm—I had to earn my living. And indeed, we began working. He had customers he knew well, and I was the stranger, the newcomer.

He introduced me to them by saying, 'This is my friend.' He didn't know my name and didn't ask, and I didn't know his name either; I just called him my friend.

We visited dozens of clients in law offices, hotels, restaurants, currency exchanges, old, abandoned doctors' clinics, and a bookstore selling Christian books next to a church. It was my first time entering this remarkable building, distinguished by its decorations. My companion, as he told me, was Christian, unlike the boy who prayed with me at dawn and left with the elegant southern woman.

By the end of the day, close to the afternoon, we had gathered a decent amount of money and went to eat together at a restaurant. I had in mind to eat a shawarma sandwich that I used to have with the limping man at that Turkish place, but I didn't know the exact location, as we usually came by car. There's a difference between discovering places by car and on foot.

After eating, we drank two bottles of Pepsi Cola. My companion then took out a cigarette similar to the ones the old man used to smoke. He lit it. I had never smoked in my life. He offered it to me, and after his insistence, I took a puff. I felt something hot and burning piercing my chest through my throat, causing me to feel breathless. I coughed repeatedly until I vomited. My friend said to me:

'This happens sometimes. You'll try again tomorrow.'

But I refused to try it again—I didn't like cigarettes, nor did I want to inhale some of the adhesives that the boys sniffed from shoe glue or solvents. There were many of them, and every day I discovered something new. I don't even know what saved me from these things—perhaps it was that old man who kept appearing in my dreams, praying for me to be a good person, which is why I made sure to never miss my prayers at the mosque.

Two weeks passed like this, and I lived on the street among the homeless boys. My bed was under a building under construction. My friend and I would sleep there and wake up every day to go to work.

I had bought a box for myself, and we started sharing the customers. We never had any problems despite the provocations from other boys and the many issues we encountered, but the elegant girl would appear from time to time and solve the complicated problems.

Unlike how she first seemed to me cold and not a welcoming person, she started to like me and began having conversations with me, in a way that indicated she was educated or attended school.

Each morning, after I had taken a short rest after dawn, I would see her before me. She came daily, gathering some of the boys and taking them with her, including the boy who was keen on praying at dawn but also smoked and did everything else, unlike me. He used to accuse me of being weak, saying it with a laugh. As the days passed, he forgot to label me that way, and one morning, before the elegant southern girl arrived, he told me:

'I'm proud of your courage. You left a comfortable life to live here.'

He was referring to my uncle's house.

He had learned my story, as there was nothing to do at night but tell stories. Everyone had their own memories, even though they were young. We would gather in a circle and talk, each telling his story, stopping at a certain point to continue the next night. Most of these stories were painful memories of the war ravaging people in the south of the country, how blood would flow and mix with the river water, and how corpses would mingle with the remnants of tree trunks in the swamps. These were stories I wouldn't have believed before, making me feel that my misery was lighter by comparison. Still, nothing drove me to want to go back.

Among the stories that occupied part of the night was the story of the elegant girl. The boys said her father was a prominent politician, and she attended an Evangelical school, spoke several languages, and was fluent in Arabic, while the others had an accent.

I learned that she took some of the boys to work in the homes of the city's elite politicians and businessmen to earn money. She also organized training programs for some to acquire life skills. I knew there was a mystery behind her, and it became clear to me.

The next day, I began to see her differently. She started to resemble my cousin's daughter in that picture I had seen—confident and steady, dark-skinned like her, with parted lips and a slightly pointed nose and a radiant forehead. The only difference was that my cousin's daughter was older. I mustered the courage to ask her that day if she could find me a job. My request wasn't genuine, as I was earning well from shining shoes, but I wanted to start a conversation with her to get to know her better—out of curiosity, for reasons I didn't understand.

She looked at me with a smile, which made her seem more beautiful, and for the first time, I felt a deep attraction to a female. Those days were marked by changes in my inner psyche and physical development. I was aware of it and could see it clearly, realizing that I was nearing manhood. She said to me:

'I knew you would ask for this. No problem.'

But she didn't respond to my request immediately. Several days passed before she came one morning and said:

'I found a job for you that will suit you perfectly.'

I eagerly asked what the job was, thinking I would probably be a servant in one of the grand houses of the city, like my friends here. But she hinted that I was special, without explaining what she meant by 'special'. Did my lighter skin tone make me special? But I wasn't the only light-skinned one here—there were dozens like me in this street, often picked up by police cars and thrown into dirty prisons, only to become servants there too.

She didn't explain the matter, so I had to accompany her on a journey that didn't last long. We got into a long car with wide doors, white in colour. The driver was a tall southern man who spoke English. We stopped at the gate of a building I recognised immediately—it was the church. We entered, where a man in white clothes was waiting for us. He greeted me by name as if he knew me and spoke to the girl in a language I didn't understand. The man had white skin, a completely white moustache, and a white skullcap. His smile was pleasant, and he seemed comforting, but I had learned in this country not to rely on the first smile, as I had from previous experiences.

The girl and the driver left, and I stayed with the man. He said to me:

'I've heard about you. You are a model of diligence and sacrifice. I know your story well.'

I didn't know how to respond, especially since I still didn't know my role or what kind of relationship would tie me to this man. But he cut to the chase, saying:

'You will work with me here and learn a lot. We have many jobs in this big building.'

At first, I was assigned to arrange the room of the man with the white skullcap, who was the main and most important figure in the church, and everyone here called him 'Father'. He was extremely kind and polite.

In the first few days, I worked during the day and returned at night to my friends in the street, who were eager to hear my story. Everyone who enters a new experience comes to tell their tale, but I preferred to remain silent or speak briefly. Over time, I reduced my visits to my friends, spending both day and night in the church, attending to the Father's needs, all the while continuing my prayers as a Muslim, without anyone objecting.

One morning, a delegation of foreigners who seemed European arrived—three men, a beautiful girl, and an elderly woman who, like me, was limping. She saw me and sympathized with me, taking a picture with me with a camera the blonde girl was carrying.

They had a translator who spoke Arabic, but the Father was fluent in their language and conversed with them skilfully.

The Father dressed me in bright clothes that day, and they took pictures of me alone, sitting next to him. I didn't know the purpose of it, nor did I ask. The delegation left, but their memory lingers with me to this day. Another delegation came later, and again, they took pictures of me, but there was no limping woman this time.

Days passed as I served the Father, organizing his small office next to the church where he would sit for long hours reading and meeting people who came in fancy cars labelled 'Diplomatic Corps'.

One afternoon, they closed off the main street next to the church, and it remained closed until late the following night. There was a heavy presence of security and police guarding the area. I understood that an important man was going to visit the church. Late at night, a noisy car arrived, led by large motorcycles ridden by men in big black helmets. I realised it was the same convoy I had seen the day I left my uncle's house for good.

I was part of the reception crew and stood there in my splendour and fine attire, looking very handsome, as I had seen in the mirror before leaving the preparation room, where a group of women had come to arrange things for me and another boy, a dark-skinned southerner I had not met before, while the elegant girl led the way holding a welcome sign. The boy and I carried a small blanket covered with fragrant flowers, atop which lay a large pair of scissors, the likes of which I had never seen before.

In those moments, I recalled my uncle's wife who once reminded me to look in the mirror while she raped me, and I felt a brief discomfort that perhaps I was being used in this situation because of my looks, even though I walked with a limp. But I didn't dwell on it for long, as the man everyone here, including our Father, bowed to entered—the President.

Contrary to the grandeur that preceded him, which suggested he might be arrogant, he was quite the opposite. He joked with everyone and laughed with them, dressed in traditional attire—a local attire and a large turban that seemed so white it looked like he was wearing it for the first time.

The event was related to a mediation effort by the Father to end the war in the south of the country, and the scissors cut a ribbon behind which a banner read 'The New Dawn', but it was a failed mediation like the others, as I learned later. The war would pause and then resume again.

That day felt like the beginning of the end of my time there. A few weeks later, the Father had changed somewhat. He hadn't lost his kindness, but he had become a bit more irritable. The delegations from diplomatic bodies had stopped coming to his office. He had stopped reading as he usually did, and his landline phone rarely rang anymore. Sometimes, he would let it ring until it stopped, no longer caring who was calling. Then one evening, a group of men in civilian clothes stormed the church building and took the Father and some of the residents, including me.

I watched as they put me into a vehicle that resembled a prison, with a closed box at the back, but it was more refined and beautiful than the police car that had previously taken us from the street. This one was a lovely blue colour. They had locked the church's outer gate with an enormous lock, the likes of which I had never seen before. The cars sped away like the wind, to where I did not know.

They took us to a house by the river, where I saw 'Our Father' being led in chains into a room. He walked with his head held high and said nothing.

Hours later, they brought me into a room with a neatly made bed and served me food. I did not know what happened to the others, and no one spoke to me until the next morning when a young man who also seemed kind arrived.

There are many kind people in this country, but one must be cautious. The young man began interrogating me, asking about my relationship with the church and the Father, and what exactly my role was.

I did not lie to him; I told him everything I knew. I wasn't sure if he believed me or if he already knew everything and this was just a silly play.

In the end, he asked me to sign at the bottom of one of the papers he had filled out with a blue pen before asking me a question he hadn't included in the written text:

'Did they ever touch you?'

I was surprised by the question. It had never happened, and I didn't ask him what he meant because it seemed clear to me. I replied:

'No, that never happened.'

He repeated with a seemingly foolish smile, his lashes fluttering as his eyes opened wide, and I couldn't see him clearly as a foggy vision had suddenly overtaken me without warning:

'Not even the Father?'

I answered immediately:

'He's a respectable man.'

He slapped me suddenly on my right cheek with a force that belied his slender appearance. Then he laughed and left, leaving the door to the room open. In those moments, I remembered my uncle and thought he might be more important than all of them. I didn't dwell on the thought as I saw a woman moving in the outer yard. I recognised her immediately as the one who clung to my uncle at the party he held at the house.

What was she doing here? I wondered if she would recognise me if she saw me. But I hoped she wouldn't see me at all. That was my wish—neither her nor my uncle. This world no longer mattered to me, but would I be able to escape it as long as I lived in this country?

Two days later, another young man came to me and said:

'We are releasing you now. Let's go.'

They took me to the blue car with the box, and it drove off for an unknown distance until I found myself in the darkness of a city street. Where was it? I had no idea. I had never discovered this place before.

They threw me to the ground like a wounded dog and sped off. I jumped up with all my strength, defying my limp, exhausted and mentally drained by the situation I found myself in without any warning.

The bag was still in my hand. I checked to make sure the Quran and the prayer beads were still inside and untouched. I had a feeling I would see the old man, my companion, who would appear now to rescue me once again from my distress, from this vast prison. But this time, my feeling was false. No one appeared. There was nothing but silence, the rustling of trees, and the distant scent of nights from my early childhood memories of my father beating my mother violently, his sweat smelling strong.

4
With the Shawarma

Now, my son, we are approaching the story of the shawarma, the tale that changed your father's life. It began precisely on that night, a night with no moon, only scattered stars, an exhausted boy, an empty street, and fragmented memories.

I closed my eyes and then opened them, rubbing them with difficulty while they were still closed, trying to make out the details of the place where I had been thrown.

It didn't seem far from the center of the big city. I understood that from the tall buildings, which exist only in this area. Yes, I recognised one of them; it's the one behind the airport—tall buildings with planes landing in their midst. Strange, but real. In this country, anything is possible.

A ghost emerged from the darkness, likely a man, a large person occupying space in the void of the night. He stopped in front of me and grabbed my hand tightly, looking directly at my face without showing any emotion.

His face was not unfamiliar; he was the stocky man who worked with the Turk in the shawarma restaurant. I remembered him; he always gave me strange looks when the limping man and I would come in.

I felt a mix of reassurance and fear, knowing I was near a place I was familiar with, and that I might be able to navigate the city once again.

The man pressed his strong body against me suddenly in the dark street, then asked me:

'Where are you going?'

I did not know what to say, as his behaviour was suspicious. In reality, I didn't know where I was going.

I stayed silent until he repeated his question, increasing the pressure on my back. I could smell the alcohol on his breath. He was drunk. I pushed him aside before finally responding:

'What do you want from me? Leave me alone.'

He twisted my arm with force, but I endured it until I managed to control his arm and push him aside like a strong elephant, sending him to the ground.

I don't know how I did it, but then I quickly ran away to escape his rudeness. However, he got up and started chasing me. Despite his heavy weight, he was surprisingly fast. Strange indeed. Just as he was about to catch me again, a hand reached out from the darkness and pushed him aside.

Another familiar face appeared; one I have told you about before. It was the Turk, the owner of the restaurant, with his neatly trimmed white beard. I hadn't expected him to recognised me in this darkness, and I was surprised when he called me by my name, which I wasn't sure he even knew before. He had never called me by my name, only referred to me as 'the boy'. He took me aside into a small house with a short iron gate surrounded by flowers that emitted a beautiful fragrance in the warm night.

The stocky man had vanished, and the Turk didn't speak to him at all. His mere presence was enough to make the man disappear into the darkness like a ghost.

I spent that night in the Turk's house, sleeping in a quiet room with no noise. It seemed like a wonderful place to stay, and I hadn't felt as mentally at ease as I did at dawn when I woke up as usual for prayer. It wasn't difficult to find the mosque; the minaret was clearly visible.

I prayed and then returned to the Turk's house, as I had nowhere else to go. The man had told me clearly:

'Sleep well, my boy, and in the morning, everything will be fine.'

Did he understand my tragedy, even though he never asked me? Maybe.

I arrived at the room after prayer… I lay down for about half an hour on a neat, elegant bed next to a small table with a vase on it. In front of me, on the wall, with the first rays of the new morning, the details of a black-and-white picture became visible—a picture of an elderly woman, hanging on the wall. She resembled the Turk. It seemed she was his mother. Or maybe his sister. It doesn't take much intelligence to figure that out.

The Turk entered, greeted me with a good morning, and placed a cup of hot coffee in front of me, along with a piece of bread and cheese. He spoke to me:

'Your friend has gone. I miss him a lot.'

It was clear he was talking about the limping man, for without him, we wouldn't have met. He didn't go on about him, but he looked at me with a bit of pity—I could sense it unless it was a false feeling, something I'd grown accustomed to in this city.

It seemed to me that he knew everything about me. He didn't say much, but as the saying goes, a single gesture is enough. He told me:

'I don't think you're happy at your uncle's house!'

He knows my uncle's house? My uncle! There's no one else who could've told him these details except the limping man. Many times, when we went to the restaurant, the limping man would stay behind to chat with the Turk, though he never cared for the fat man. He despised him. Once, he called him despicable when he caught him staring at me.

I never knew, not even once, the content of their conversations. It seemed I was a part of those discussions that are now left behind with the man who has gone and left me alone. I felt pain remembering him. Sometimes, I'm sensitive, and my tears flow for the slightest reasons, and the Turk saw that.

He saw me almost choking, so he said:

'Don't worry about the future... If you need any help, I'll provide it. The limping man had virtues I admired.'

He continued:

'You're also a good person and deserve a lot... You're...'

He was about to say something but stammered or left it unfinished; I don't know... He suddenly stopped talking.

With the birth of the new day, I thanked him, deciding to return to my friends on that street, where I would resume my job as a shoe shiner. I told him this, and he wished me success in my journey in life, then said to me:

'I have a small request from you.'

I leaned in to hear his request, and he said in his comforting way:

'Come by every morning to shine my shoes... and greet your uncle.'

He temporarily bid me farewell with a look that seemed sad to me... before I returned to my friends, who had gathered around to hear my story... what had happened to me since I left them.

They told me that the elegant girl had disappeared for days... and I understood that it might have something to do with the arrest of the father and the closure of the church. The boys were talking about more people arriving from the war zone, and that the battles had intensified terribly in the past two days.

One could know the details of what was happening in the south by listening to the news here, as journalists were spreading out to gather information, as my shoe-shining friend informed me, warning me not to talk to anyone I didn't trust, because the area was being watched, and any word from me that displeased them could land me back in prison.

He didn't tell me who he meant by 'they' but I understood... My life experiences were expanding, and I began to understand the landscape of life in this country since that moment when the old man on the train was talking about weak faith.

Every morning, I would pass by the Turk, whom I had started calling 'uncle'. I would shine his shoes. I gained some good experience with different shoe brands, and through that, I learned about their owners and their preferences. I could distinguish between imported and locally made shoes. My uncle the Turk's shoes were strange to me at first; later, I learned they were made in Antalya, Turkey, blue in colour with cotton laces, but very light. The leather looked artificial, but it was one hundred percent natural. This particular shoe needed a special polish, so I had to rely on the expertise of my small shoe-shining friend.

My uncle, the Turk, was generous, giving me more money than the actual price for shining his shoes. I passed by dozens of people daily, some paying a decent amount, but many just paid the standard rate... a quarter of a pound. They wouldn't even be kind to you except on certain days when their faces would suddenly become cheerful without any known reason. Not everyone reveals their secrets, but there are also those who talk too much.

I would listen to everyone without complaint, as my job required it. But my uncle was different; he didn't speak much. He would sit on the chair at the entrance, extending his leg and resting it on a raised stone on the ground.

I would start my work at seven in the morning, never being late. I understood that punctuality and commitment to time were the most important things for success in work. That was one of my uncle's pieces of advice when he felt like talking, especially after I was late a few times in the early days... maybe a lot... He said to me:

'If you want to start right, be punctual.'

That became a goal, a banner I carried in my heart. Every day, I would listen to his wisdom. He didn't intentionally give advice, but his way of talking was like that. His life experience spoke for him... And I felt he was keen for me to become a real man by relying on myself. He once told me:

'If you want to move forward, never look back.'

I had a feeling that he had a secret life like mine... even though my story was no longer a secret to him... as I understood over time, the limping man had told him everything. I was eager to know the reason that brought him from Turkey to my country to work here... What are the reasons that make a person migrate and start working in another country and succeed at it... So many questions I wanted to answer.

In the recent past, the limping man would answer some of my questions... He would fill me with enthusiasm and the desire for more questions and to bravely explore life. Today, my uncle, the Turk, makes me feel positive things, but I'm too shy to ask him questions... And I became addicted to coming every morning... to listen, learn, and become more precise in my work.

During the previous period, I moved to live in a small house, which was just one room, with my shoe-shining friend. It wasn't a rented house... It was abandoned... located on a main street in the city center, accessible through a narrow alley... No one noticed this house or saw it unless they had been there before... It was one of the discoveries of my shoe-shining friend.

We lived there after we fixed it up well and repaired the roof so it wouldn't let rainwater in during the fall. We painted the walls blue... and drew figures resembling us... We tested our drawing skills... and bought a small wardrobe where we kept our clothes... We finally started changing clothes every day or two at most, as there was a lot of dust in the city. In the past, we almost died from our own stench... We had a small bathroom without pipes, and we would bring water to it from a nearby fountain in the middle of the alley. Its water was slightly cold... We didn't know its source, but we treated it as a blessing from God.

My uncle, the Turk, used to notice the changes in my life... and I used to tell him in a brief about what was happening. He understood life well and didn't need me to explain much, as a single hint would be enough for him to grasp everything as if he had gone through similar experiences to mine. He got to know my shoe-shining friend and my roommate... that boy from the faraway forests... and he advised me to take good care of him... just as he advised him. He told us:

'You two are a small model of your plundered country's unity.'

We weren't concerned with the political struggles and what goes on in the tall buildings in the city... how they ignite or extinguish wars or disturb the lives of ordinary people.

Sometimes I would recall my experience with the church and the father, feeling nostalgic for those days. It now seems to me a wonderful and beloved experience. Our father was a good and patriotic man, but life has its own twists.

At the same time, I feared that the experience with the father might repeat with my uncle, the Turk, that I might lose him one day. Even though the man didn't seem concerned with politics, politicians, elections, or wars... I learned over time that they don't leave anyone alone... This pronoun 'they' that people often used in the street to keep quiet about the subject. But everyone knew exactly who was meant.

My friend would sometimes go to pray at the church, which they reopened, but the father didn't reappear. As for me, I would pray at the mosque. No one talked to the other about their religious rituals.

My friend continued smoking but never smoked in the room to avoid bothering me. He knew I didn't like the smell of smoke... And as the weeks passed our relationship grew stronger, and we distanced ourselves from the world of street boys and their daily lives, but from time to time, we would go to them with some gifts we bought with our surplus money.

During that period, I began to rediscover some of my old hobbies, like reading a book, while my friend enjoyed painting. He bought an easel and some paper and started practicing his hobby in the evenings after we managed to secretly connect electricity to our room from a neighbouring building.

We would wake up at dawn, even if we had stayed up late. We do our work with sincerity and love and now our lives have other pleasures besides relentless work.

I would, as usual, visit my Turkish uncle, never being late. But then came that morning when I arrived and found he wasn't there.

The fat man was standing there, trying to flirt with me, as if seizing the opportunity, but in this time in broad daylight he was with his full conscious not drunk, seemed more humorous than offensive, and I laughed a lot that day instead of being annoyed.

I realised that the man had another dimension to him. I usually didn't talk to him, ever since that night when the Turk had chased him away from me. Since then, he had dealt with me cautiously, knowing that my relationship with his master had gradually strengthened.

That morning, instead of answering my question 'Where is my uncle?' he replied:

'Hey, sweet boy!'

He said it in front of people without a care, as if taking advantage of his master's absence to be bold, yet he was gentle and amusing.

One of the customers, who I often saw coming every morning for shawarma, whispered to me:

'He's good with words, but he doesn't do anything... he owns nothing.'

I thought to myself, laughing, 'It seems my uncle knows this secret, which is why he keeps him around.'

After he had exhausted his dirty jokes, playing with the customers, and enjoying their comments about him, he finally answered my question:

'Your uncle travelled and will be back in a few days... I'm the king here now. Come to shine my shoes.'

I thought he was joking. I had never polished his shoes before. I knew that he didn't wear the kind of shoes that needed shining; he preferred traditional shoes made from leopard skin, which didn't need polish.

In this line of work, the first thing I notice about someone is their footwear. But this time, I missed it because the fat man had distracted me with his funny talk. I noticed that he was wearing blue shoes with laces, perhaps his master's shoes, but they were a different size. The Turk's feet were long and slender, while the fat man's feet were very wide and full of fat. He seemed to eat a lot.

I sat on the ground to start my work, and he sat on his master's chair, pretending to play his role, though not very convincingly. When I finished polishing the shoes, he pulled out one pound from his pocket and stuffed it into my shirt pocket. The customers laughed heartily as they watched the entertaining scene.

The place suddenly fell silent when a dignified lady walked in, looking to be in her fifties. She was wearing a green striped blouse and a pure white skirt just above her knees. Her face was radiant but very stern, freshly washed with a strong fragrance, and her lips were small and red. She was of medium height, and it seemed she had been beautiful in her youth.

I guessed that she was the Turk's wife or a relative. Although I had spent that night at his house, I hadn't seen anyone other than that picture hanging on the wall. I didn't know if the man had a wife, children, or relatives here. I didn't know, and I hadn't asked, and it wasn't my place to ask.

As soon as the Turkish lady entered, the fat man transformed into a very respectful person. I had come to understand people here very well—they were experts at acting. He now seemed meek and very polite in front of the Turkish lady.

She glanced around the place, ensuring everything was in order. The customers were also stealing glances at her, showing respect. She sat on a large chair inside, under the air conditioner that was blasting into the small inner hall of the restaurant. She grabbed a bunch of ledgers and began flipping through them, making notes with a pencil. It seemed she was reviewing the daily accounts. I decided to leave before finding out where my uncle had gone.

The next day, I returned, but the master still wasn't there, meaning he hadn't returned yet. The fat man was more polite, seeming to expect the Turkish lady to arrive at any moment, preparing in advance.

He was generous with me that day, not pretending to be the master and making me polish his shoes. Instead, he asked me to help him polish the floors in the inner hall because the lady was not satisfied with the restaurant's cleanliness. I didn't mind and did the job well. I like to be thorough in my work and to love what I do; it's one of my Turk uncle's teachings.

After that, another task awaited me: to write some banners. The fat man asked if my handwriting was good, and I replied that it was. The signs were paper, listing the prices and welcoming phrases. He told me the lady had requested it. I did the job well and stepped back to admire the neat, brown-coloured writing in bold gel pen script.

When the lady arrived, the place became quieter. She had a more fragrant scent that morning compared to the previous day. She carefully examined the banners, and I saw joy in her eyes. My handwriting was indeed beautiful, but I hadn't realised it before or used it for anything useful. She also inspected the brightly polished tiles.

She asked the fat man who had done such a fine job, and he pointed to me. I felt embarrassed and lowered my head. She said to me:

'Come here, boy… What's your name, and what do you do?'

That's a long story, one I couldn't possibly summarize for her. Should I tell her that I ran away from my father's house because I hated living there, that I love my mother and siblings, but I can't go back? I can't even say for sure that I hate my father. I sacrificed love for something else—a mysterious adventure in my life that I will eventually reach, a specific and important outcome. That feeling and hope nurtured in me by the limping man.

Sometimes, in my solitude when I lie down to sleep in that room I crafted with my friend the shoe-shiner, I feel like a harsh creature made of strange clay. Sometimes, I feel like I'm wronging my family and should return to them, but I can't. There's a voice inside me that chases me, telling me no, telling me to listen only to my inner voice, the feeling deep within my soul that I should be myself, no one else.

I remember the day I was among the street children, before I became a good shoe-shiner and before I went to church. A man in a white suit came by, never giving his name, carrying a large notebook. He would sit with the boys, talk to them, and write things down in his notebook. I was one of those who sat with him. He asked me why I was here, and I told him:

'I want to be myself... I don't like life at our home.'

After hearing my story and writing down what he wrote, he said to me:

'Do you think that's enough? Look around you; some of these boys have no families, no parents... You have a family, a mother with a kind heart.'

He continued listing what seemed like logical and convincing reasons, but my heart was beating to a different rhythm that I couldn't control.

The image of the man with the bag appeared before me, telling me not to let this man sitting in front of me disturb or confuse my journey in life.

His voice spoke in the limping man's voice, telling me:

'The braves in this world are not troubled by emotions... Emotion is necessary, but it's not everything.'

This seemed contradictory to my daily prayers and my commitment to them. I knew that prayer purified the soul, but my purified soul thought only of the future, never looking back to yesterday. I felt no pangs of conscience. Even my mother's image seemed hazy to me now; I couldn't bring it into focus, even as tears uncontrollably welled up in my eyes.

My shoe-shiner friend told me:

'They say he's a psychiatrist who wants to treat us... They claim we suffer from psychological cracks.'

I learned from the boys that there were many like him, who would come by from time to time. Some called themselves academics, specialists, or doctors in psychiatric hospitals, others in private clinics conducting research studies for foreign organizations. The boys here knew everything; they knew that many people were interested in them for ignoble reasons, for money, not for any other purpose. Some of these visitors with their notebooks were sometimes beaten and thrown out, as the boys knew whom to respect, whom to value, and whom to kick out.

The psychiatrist's story stirred some temporary knots within me, making me feel like an incomplete being or that I suffered from some sort of defect. The man said to me after closing his notebook and looking at me intently:

'You suffer from a mysterious illness, my boy... It's not autism or schizophrenia... I can't explain it; I need more analysis and examination. Will you come with me tomorrow to my lab so we can figure it out together?'

I shouted at him:

'I'm not sick!'

I was surprised that a man who called himself a specialist would address a young boy this way. It seemed he was the one with a psychological problem, ashamed to confront this mysterious illness. I, too, as soon as he walked away, started screaming hysterically, clearly showing that I might actually be sick, unable to face myself with it.

I moved away, leaving him to talk to himself like a madman. A madman holding a large notebook with a colourful cover and a pen tucked behind his left ear, like a carpenter, sitting on a stone in the street, perhaps reflecting on his past or nothing at all.

The lady sat me next to her... My Turkish aunt seemed kind, as she did from the very first moment. But as I had learned, I should never rush to conclusions... because the opposite could happen... The inhabitants of this city often lack a conscience. She ran her hand through my long, curly hair, which I rarely cut or wash. I had let it grow naturally since I left the town, where there was no school principal to check for lice, making a haircut mandatory. The lice had left my hair entirely without warning, suddenly disappearing one night.

She also kissed my cheek, and I felt a strange longing for my mother's embrace, but I held back my tears. She pushed me back a bit and stood, looking at me. She was talking to herself, unconcerned with the people in the restaurant. I heard her say, 'It's him... It's like him...' And I didn't understand the meaning. What was the story exactly? Who was this person she was talking about? Perhaps I resembled someone, a boy in her life. She asked me:

'Which northern tribes do you belong to?'

A tribe... I don't know... I had never heard my father talk about a specific tribe we belonged to. Sometimes my mother would say our family came from the Egyptian countryside... My mother's skin was lighter than my father's... My father didn't know where he came from or where he was going, and he didn't have time to talk about such matters. I didn't know the answer, so I told her:

'I don't know, ma'am... I don't know.'

The fat man intervened without being asked, eavesdropping on the conversation between me and the lady. He clarified:

'She means do you have relatives with roots in Turkey?'

I started to understand the matter. I almost resembled a Turkish boy in her life... That might be true... or maybe not... I had no answer. This resemblance suggested that my relatives had roots there... From what I knew of history from school, our country was colonized by the Turks a hundred years ago, who left after a war led by a revolutionary called Al-Mahdi. They tell us this in schools... And that some

Turkish families stayed, married, and lived on to this day... Perhaps that's what she meant.

I didn't take much time to analyse or try to discover the connection between me and the person I resembled... until the fat man suddenly nudged me strongly, but gently, on my back, alerting me to look toward the wall. There was a surprise I didn't expect... A large picture was hanging on the wall, similar to the one I had seen in the Turkish man's house in the room where I slept... A boy stood confidently, leaning on a staff decorated at the top with an ornamented ball, wearing a white cap and a beautiful white suit. It was me... Not just a resemblance... It was exactly like me... Why hadn't I noticed this picture before... if it had been here all these months?

The lady also stood, shifting her gaze between me and the picture. Tears flowed from her eyes, and she embraced me tightly, saying:

'My son... My son.'

I couldn't hold back and cried with her. I realised the matter was related to her son in the picture. He was her son and the Turkish man's son... Was that why he had been caring for me for so long?

My confusion remained because I hadn't noticed this picture if it had been there before, and why hadn't the limping man noticed it and pointed it out to me? I didn't think he would have missed it, and because the question bothered me, I asked the fat man later:

'Has it been there for a long time?'

He smiled and said:

'For a long time... How long is long? A day or two... A year... Two years... Or do you mean since he died?'

He laughed outrageously without answering my question and I said:

'So he's dead... How long has he been dead?... Oh... that's why she...'

The fat man interrupted me and didn't let me speak, as the lady had left. He had returned to his rudeness especially since the shop was almost empty of customers at midday.

He nearly pressed against my back again. I punched him hard and fled from him and the shop to the room, where I felt an unjustified psychological exhaustion. Perhaps the Turkish lady's emotions affected me or it was nostalgia for my family, especially my mother. She must have missed me just as this lady missed her son.

I began to wonder how he died. Did he die as a boy my age? Did he die from an illness, or how did he die?

I drifted off to sleep deeply. I wished I could see my old friend, the one with the bag... to see the lice crawling on his white hair, his friend... but that didn't happen. I didn't wake up until dawn. my friend was finishing a new painting. This time he had painted me. It was as if it were me or as if I were the Turkish boy whose picture was hanging in the restaurant.

An idea came to me to ask him for the painting to give it to the lady; I knew he would give it to me. And that's what happened.

I rushed to the restaurant, and my Turkish uncle had returned from his trip. He welcomed me warmly. I gave him the painting. He looked at it with childlike joy and thanked me. I told him that my friend had painted it and that I had intended to give it to the lady who was here yesterday. He said:

'Whether it's for her or for me, we both thank you and your friend.'

He made a phone call from the landline to the home, sharing the good news with his wife, as he described it. We chatted afterward, and I told him the story of my surprise with the picture I hadn't seen before. He replied simply that this is normal in a person's life. He told me:

'Many things are around us, and we don't notice them… until the right time… just like life and a person's experiences in general in the world.'

I didn't ask him whether he loved me because I resembled his son or if he loved me because he loved me, but I chose to leave that question because it would embarrass him. The man is kind to me and there's no doubt that if he doesn't love me like his son, he at least appreciates me a great deal.

I was still eager to hear his story… the reason he came to our country… and the story of his son, which had emerged as a fascinating matter to me. It now concerned me more because this boy seemed as if he were me, and I kept staring at his picture again.

He was a bit taller than me. His moustache was small or just beginning to grow. His eyes were strikingly beautiful. They radiated something strange as if he were looking at something far away, thinking about it when the picture was taken.

The fat man was watching me secretly, clearly annoyed by the master's arrival. His discomfort was palpable and didn't require more than a pair of eyes to see it.

I spent half of my day in the restaurant, organizing some things at my uncle's request. He had learned what I had done during his absence, praising my work. He discovered that I could help out here somehow. He probably knew that but was waiting for the right moment to say:

'Come work with us.'

The fat man was the thread that led to that, even if his intentions were not noble.

My Turkish uncle told me:

'From today, you'll work with us here in the restaurant… This request is long overdue.'

He spoke with great politeness, as if I were the one asking him to work with me. The fat man was still sneaking glances at me, and I couldn't quite tell how he felt about his master's decision. Was he pleased with it or not?

I left at the end of the day to my shared room with my friend and told him that from today, I would have to leave the shoe-polishing job and that my uncle had arranged for me to work with him. He was happy for what had happened, and I thanked him greatly that the painting he had gifted me might have been a direct reason for what happened, but I assured him that I wouldn't leave my lodging here with him, as my uncle hadn't brought up the subject, and I would currently apologise if he offered. I wouldn't leave my friend alone.

At the dawn of a new day, the first day of my work with my Turkish uncle in the restaurant, I had bid farewell to the world of shoes, though not entirely. I made sure to polish my uncle's shoes every morning and sometimes the fat man's shoes, which he wore occasionally when the master was away for reasons I didn't know. He sometimes travelled out of the country and returned… and I wasn't one to ask; I had learned not to interfere in matters not told to me.

The new job was, of course, different from my previous one. At first, I felt like I was entering a field in which I had no experience… My expertise was with shoes: polishing them, knowing their colours and sizes, and where they were made. Now I had to learn about types of meat, what's suitable for making shawarma, and what isn't. How the fire should be at a certain level to cook the meat to the right tenderness, making it taste delicious as the customers say.

My first teacher was the master himself, and the fat man didn't withhold information when my uncle was present. In front of him, he seemed calm and obedient, acting like a noble and well-mannered man to the fullest extent.

Over time, I came to understand that the master was aware of the fat man's temperament. He knew his weaknesses but was fully aware of his strength as a skilled cook and a maker of outstanding shawarma. And after having trained under him many years ago, my uncle kept him around and tolerated some of his excesses and shortcomings.

Most importantly, the fat man, to this day, seemed more verbal than practical in his personal behaviour and his constant winking with his eyes, whether with me or some of the young men who come to the shop and whom he expresses admiration for, making them the subject of jokes in the absence of my uncle.

As days, weeks, and months went by, I became fully immersed in the work. I would wake up early from the shared room to reach the restaurant. I had a copy of the shop's key, so I would open it, clean the floors, wipe and polish the walls and windows, and receive the meat and vegetables from the suppliers who arrived early. Then I would arrange them in the large refrigerator in the internal storage.

I had memorized the layout of the shop, which I had never seen before. There was a large internal room with a bed where the fat man would lie down for his nap, but in the evening there was no room for rest as the work was intense and the customers numerous. People of various appearances came, including Sudanese and other expatriates living in the country. There were also customers in diplomatic vehicles, like those who used to visit my father at the church. Hence, some faces were familiar to me from the European diplomats and foreign organization staff.

The fat man had started to reconcile with me and accept the situation. I can't say for certain that he had a problem with me, except for his weakness, especially when he got drunk late at night, and he only drank after finishing his work. My uncle didn't care about this matter, seeing it as a personal issue. But as I learned, everything becomes clear over time; days reveal the obscure details.

Over time, I discovered that the fat man had other weaknesses that my uncle was unaware of. If he had known, he wouldn't have tolerated them. I doubt that. It was difficult for me to intervene and be a tattletale, so I had to be patient. I learned from my uncle himself that no matter how strong your relationship with someone, you should not rush to tell everything to others, especially if it concerns other people and not yourself. Your own self is your own affair.

What I observed and confirmed through repetition was that the fat man was not honest. He was stealing from the savings box, especially when the boss was absent, hiding the money in his pocket. He was in the habit of doing this and would hide to avoid being seen by me. It seemed that in the past, he found opportunities to steal because there was no one to oversee the shop.

The fat man didn't need to betray his employer. He received a high salary by the country's standards, and he personally informed me that there was no one more generous than this man to work for.

During some free time, when we would sit and relax in the internal room, he would gossip about his life and experiences. He shared things he had never dared to say before, including his weakness. However, he never admitted to me that he was a thief. His image of my uncle was ideal as a rare person in this world filled with evildoers instead of good people.

He would lie on the floor or sometimes on a plastic mat or on the bed, talking to me as if he were talking to himself. I didn't find him as wise as the limping man or that his experience was fascinating to me, but I learned that every person, if given the chance, has something to say, according to my uncle's wisdom, or something they do.

I thought there might come a day when he would confess to the theft. I had this feeling, so I told myself I should leave things to time and stick to the principles my uncle advised. So I continued to observe daily and saw the thefts recurring.

It became clear to me that the amounts were not small as I had initially thought. I had judged that the extent of the theft should reflect on the thief's appearance, but this theory didn't hold true for the fat man. It seemed he was saving this money or investing it in something I didn't know about.

Eventually, one day I decided to tell my uncle. I couldn't bear to see the kind man being stolen from, and before I told him, I decided to confront the fat man and seized the opportunity when we were alone in the room during the nap time.

The fat man had just finished his noon prayers, and as soon as he completed his supplications, I sat close to him and told him I wanted to discuss something important with him. He usually didn't care much as he seemed to have nothing important in his life. But as soon as I mentioned that the topic was about his theft, he suddenly became agitated. He hadn't expected me to use that term so directly. He said:

'Do you know that I steal from the boss?'

I confronted him firmly, seeing the weakness in his eyes:

'Don't you have any shame? The man is so generous with you, and you say he is the most generous you've known.'

He interrupted me, kneeling on the ground as if he wanted to kiss my hand and he said:

'Please, he must not know about this. He knows a lot about me, my faults, but he doesn't know that I steal from him.'

I felt sympathy for him, especially as he assured me he wouldn't repeat it. I warned him:

'If I see anything again, I won't hesitate to tell my uncle.'

In the days following that encounter, he showed commitment, at least as far as I could see. What happened beyond that I had no concrete evidence for.

The confrontation with the fat man strengthened my relationship with him, at least as I saw it. Although before that day he had started to talk about his weaknesses in front of the boys, despite admitting that he couldn't do anything and that some customers knew about it.

The aftermath of that day made him open his heart to me about events and occurrences that could only be shared with someone he fully trusted. He told me he felt a deep guilt because he had killed someone one day!

I was in the presence of a fugitive from justice. He recounted that his past wasn't encouraging to narrate—how he had engaged in theft for years in a distant country in the north. He started his life by robbing shops in the market, sneaking in and taking something to sell, then repeating the process. He had never been caught by the police or discovered by anyone. Until that night when he killed a man because he had discovered him trying to steal from a shop in the dark by climbing from above and rummaging through the roof. This was a new skill he had acquired and had executed it accurately and successfully several times.

He told a story that seemed like a fantasy to me. He showed no emotions—he was the same person who joked with the customers, the same person who tried to cling to my back, the man who is sometimes weak and sometimes strong.

He continued to narrate what happened that night, he described how he smashed the man's head with the pickaxe he used to break into the roof of the shop. This happened about thirty years ago or slightly less. Now, at nearly fifty-five, as he estimated, he continued to breathe and then sighed, as if feeling the pain or weakness of that unforgivable old event.

His confession to me meant that I had discovered the dark side of his world. But he said to me:

'If I didn't truly love and trust you, I wouldn't have shared my story.'

I looked at him jokingly, although I felt a bit afraid of an unfinished tale, and I said to him:

'Don't you fear me? Are you sure I...?'

He looked at me with eyes reflecting deep pain, a picture of a person who seems beautiful from within despite everything. He broke our silence by saying with a tone of sadness unlike his usual joking manner:

'What have I done? Wasn't one of the prophets a killer?'

We were silent for a long time, then resumed our work. He spent the rest of the day more lively as if he was starting to love life or discover it for the first time. Even my uncle noticed this and remarked:

'You look youthful today, mashallah.'

He smiled and moved the large knife he was using to cut the meat vertically, preparing a batch of sandwiches for the customers who had doubled in recent weeks after we had rearranged many things.

My presence in the shop had an impact, and I felt that without appearing proud of what was happening. My personal ambitions were far beyond that. My uncle rarely praised me. I didn't doubt that he appreciated my work; I had begun to understand his way of working—persisting in doing good things and improving your skills without expecting thanks from anyone. True appreciation relates to how you feel you are doing your duty, loving what you do, and being happy with it.

The next day, during the nap time, after we had prayed together I and the fat man, and I was the imam, at his insistence, he shared more disturbing details about that old night. He talked about how he noticed someone was following him like his shadow. He put aside his fears, climbed the brick wall, clinging to the tips of his toes, until he reached the roof of the shops. He identified the specific location where he needed to dig to enter below. Everything was done quickly; he was not as fat as he was now.

'I was very light. Thieves need to be light or they fail in their mission.'

There was no moon in the sky. The weather was very cold, but he didn't feel the harshness of the cold. He continued his mission until he spotted the man who had been following him. He approached him, tried to pounce on him, and found him resisting him fiercely. They clashed on the roof, and the simple palm frond and dom palm leaf-covered roof of the shop shook. In seconds, the suspended space would collapse, and they would be together in the middle of the shop. He struck the man with a pickaxe, the sharp head embedded in the man's head, crushing it completely. He left him bleeding and unable to scream, and vanished into the darkness.

The town spoke the next day about the murder of his cousin. He had killed his cousin without realizing it, or maybe he knew. He told me:

'I couldn't see anything. I was poisoned by a malicious germ. When a person commits murder, he no longer sees anything. Some people think murder is difficult, but on the contrary, it's very easy to kill a person. It doesn't require courage. Brave people don't kill. Only cowards get rid of their enemies by killing them and then spend the rest of their lives facing their fears. That's not accurate. Only two days and life returns to normal with him. That's what happened to me.'

The police conducted investigations and used all the means they knew. At the moment I felt I might be the target,

I had already fled the town and reached the big city to start my new life. I asked him:

'But didn't they chase you?'

'We are relatives after all. When they learned of the matter, it was after many years—nine years, I think. The file was closed permanently. And those who knew about it, in reality, were only us. His mother died when he was young, and his father disappeared since his childhood. He left and never returned to the town. So, I am the closest person to him and my siblings. You know that in this country, everything runs by the law of money. The story ended, as I later learned, with a small piece of land acquired by the investigator, and the investigators started on other cases, looking for new bribes.'

The fat man did not return to the town afterward. He spent years in the big city, working in various jobs until he settled with the Turkish man. For over twenty years, he worked here in the shawarma shop. He became part of the shop's character and descriptions for those who came for the first time.

He had finished recounting those harsh memories and showed little interest in what lay beyond. He told me:

'What matters is tomorrow. God knows what will be. I don't fear the past.'

Despite this, he was not afraid. He was fierce in facing the days, spending his free hours on things that brought him joy in the world, like drinking wine or spying on boys and young men in the city streets. His greatest pleasure was to catch someone and let him go immediately, within seconds.

He would tell me this without the slightest shame. I became a confidant to him, though sometimes I could not fully trust him. I felt he was imaginary, inventing stories. This feeling would come over me without tangible proof. The story of him killing someone seemed fabricated to me. I had to believe it until proven otherwise.

I preferred to remain silent about my thoughts concerning him, as I learned from my uncle that one should not clutter their mind with unhelpful things that do not assist in shaping their life better. I convinced myself that I was not achieving any benefit by wasting time deeply thinking about the fat man's puzzle. In the past, the limping man also had a history, but I didn't concern myself with it. I needed to be wiser as I moved forward despite maturity in life. I reached this conclusion with myself.

Days passed. I began to be late on work frequently. Sometimes I had to sleep at the shop in the internal room. It had an old air conditioner that worked with water, making the place cool and pleasant to sleep after a long day. And so I rarely saw my friend in the shared room.

Of course, my staying at the shop was based on my uncle's advice. He suggested that instead of walking to my residence, it would be better for me to stay here. The fat man was unaware of this. Perhaps he might think of some trick if he knew I was here alone. However, he would inevitably discover it one day, for nothing in the world remains hidden forever.

My friend visited me from time to time. He was reproachful, and I told him that work was becoming overwhelming, and we must strive for tomorrow. This is my principle. He would listen to my words and then repeat them sarcastically, as usual:

'Striving for tomorrow...'

I felt guilty for being absent from him. Hence, I apologised to my uncle for two days, during which I had returned early until I met my friend, and we spent the night together. We went to the cinema and watched an Indian film about children being kidnapped from villages and sold to masters in cities to become their servants. The masters treated them harshly, and their families did it for money. We discussed the film's idea together. We were convinced it was realistic but with some exaggerations. We had a fair ability for evaluation and critique.

My friend was smoking a cigarette while drinking Coca-Cola, and I was drinking hibiscus juice in the same way the limping man used to. It wasn't my usual way of drinking, but the limping man's ghost crossed my mind and made me do it.

We walked a long distance until we reached near the river. Foreign workers were building a new bridge across the water from north to south, next to the old iron bridge that the train had once crossed, bringing me here. The river was tumultuous, as the flood season was approaching, but the bridge workers paid no attention and continued their work. My friend told me an incident that happened two days ago when they poured an Italian worker inside a large concrete column. They had no time to retrieve him after discovering his dire fate too late.

My friend knew many news items that I had missed in recent days. Shawarma customers' concerns were different from those my friends in the street paid attention to and discussed.

A week later, we were making adjustments in the restaurant. Work stopped for only two days. Wall and floor restorers arrived, and we bought new tables. The fat man was energetically doing his job as if he had just been born. My friend had come to make drawings on the walls. I suggested the idea to my uncle, who agreed. Among the drawings was a large, distinctive mural occupying a quarter of the wall, featuring the boy who resembled me—the Turkish boy who died, whose secret I still do not know.

My uncle would occasionally glance at the mural as it was being completed by my friend's skilled hands. This time, it was not inspired by me but rather a real image my friend used, which had already been hanging in the restaurant. Although it was in black and white, the new mural appeared in vibrant colours on the wall. Everyone who saw it would look at me and say:

'This is you...'

I wouldn't answer yes or no. Many people began to believe that I was the Turkish's son and he would tell anyone who asked about the mural that it was my son without clarifying the difference between his real and fake son.

That evening after a long day at work, Auntie had come to the shop to see her son's mural. She stood looking at it from a distance, then approached with tears in her eyes.

Until that day, the story of the boy who resembled me was unclear to me. That evening, I learned a little about it—not the entire story. She pointed at the drawing, unable to stop the deep sadness within her. She told me, holding me without considering her actions:

'He was beautiful and handsome, as if you were twins. That's why I loved you, boy...'

She preferred to call me 'boy', and I liked this term because I felt it came from her sincere depths. She sat on the floor, half her body, holding my hand, looking intently at the painting while telling me:

'They killed him. It was a painful day, my son. I couldn't bear the news. It's God's will; what could we have done...'

I waited to hear the rest of the painful story while my uncle had disappeared. Perhaps he went for some purpose or didn't want to live these moments to avoid increasing the sorrow. The fat man had also disappeared. I think he was in the internal store arranging some things. Meanwhile, my friend had also vanished, preferring to leave us alone, me and Auntie.

She continued as if talking to herself:

'Bullets were pouring from unknown locations in the street, close to here. The masked soldiers entered at night, and during the day, they wreaked havoc in the city. They called them mercenaries. They called themselves heroes. The president announced on the radio that they wanted to overthrow the regime by any means.'

These events were not far off, as far as I knew. I was in the town at that time. My father had come back home in the daytime, performing his daily ritual of shouting and beating my mother, and me as well, before talking about the chaos occurring in the capital and how the streets were filled with corpses. My mother was afraid for her brother's fate. My uncle looked at her and said:

'Don't be foolish. Those who die are usually common people. Scoundrels like him don't die.'

My mother was angry at my uncle's description of her brother as a scoundrel, a term she heard frequently along with other descriptions.

Now, Auntie was shedding more pain as she cried for her son. She said only a few words and did not share all the details. To me, the story seems incomplete. I wanted to know more—not just about how it happened, but also about the son himself. What was he like? Did he resemble me in the way he talked or walked with a limp? I don't think so.

My aunt got up after taking one last look at the painting, just as my uncle returned, followed by the fat man. It was as if they had perfectly timed their return together. So, the fat man hadn't been in the storeroom.

My uncle asked me to accompany my aunt home because she was exhausted and needed someone to look after her on the way. We walked together; the house wasn't far. My uncle didn't like cars and preferred walking, as did his wife. They often walked to the downtown markets to buy household necessities at the end of the week, usually early in the morning, so my uncle could return to work by noon. The shop operated day and night, with no breaks—a very exhausting routine. But for me, it was enjoyable, and I had gotten used to it and loved it.

After the shop was renovated and reorganized, it marked the beginning of a new phase of intensive work, especially with the increase in customers. My dedication to work grew, as did my love for my uncle, who gave me a great opportunity to prove my abilities and test myself. It made me realize that I could be a successful person in life.

I remembered the wisdom of the limping man: schools aren't everything. That's why I never thought of going back to school, and my uncle never discussed it with me. I was learning the details of everything and realised that the steps to success in any work require delving into and scrutinizing the finer details. The world we live in is made up of very specialized fields, and a truly successful person knows how to master a craft or job, reaching secrets that no one else knows. I don't claim that the previous period was enough for me to acquire those secrets, but I certainly learned many things that would be useful in the days to come.

Although life was routine and repetitive, the joy I found in work removed any sense of boredom. My uncle taught me:

'The laws of the universe are based on routine. The sun rises every day, sets, and then returns to the same cycle. Trees grow, wither, and die, only to be replaced by new trees. Rivers rise, overflow, then dry up, only to repeat the cycle again. That's how life is, my son. The only real secret to happiness is finding a particular talent that allows you to live happily within this routine'

Every day, I learned something new. I loved discovering things I didn't know before and refining my skills. The work wasn't just about making shawarma, preparing it, or the magical spice mix my uncle personally oversaw, which distinguished our shop from any competitor. It was also about what my uncle called 'the chemistry of the soul' as he explained it:

'If you don't do things with a genuine love for what you're doing, they won't turn out well. That's a secret many who try to bypass the laws of existence don't understand.'

Over time, I began to understand that something as simple as measuring the right amount of salt isn't just about taste, but also about the feeling of the salt itself that comes with sprinkling it into the meat. I memorized these lessons from my uncle by heart and applied them. He would sometimes praise my intelligence, but not too much, for fear it would spoil me. He'd say:

'Praise is necessary, like salt, but not to the extent that it spoils the food.'

As I carried out my daily duties, I felt like a bird without wings, soaring in a high sky. I was filled with strong feelings of love for the world, and I had almost completely freed myself from the past, living in my new world.

I loved my uncle and his wife, and even the fat man, who had become my friend. Despite not telling new stories about his past crimes or that terrifying story about death, I still believed that the man sometimes confused facts with the fantasies in his mind. What mattered to me was that I enjoyed listening to him, even his vulgar gestures in front of customers when my uncle was away. I began to understand why my uncle kept him around.

One day, I discovered a secret about the thefts the fat man had committed. My uncle told me during a daytime conversation about life and people's mistakes:

'I know he's stealing from me, but he steals out of love. That's the difference, my son, between someone who steals out of envy or malice and someone who steals out of affection.'

My uncle's philosophy in life was somewhat strange. I don't think he was trying to justify events and actions; he was sincere in his words. I never saw him engage in deception; he simply spoke his beliefs without waiting for others to accept or reject them. He continued to tell me:

'When he does this, he feels a small pleasure that makes me happier, which reflects on his work, and he performs better the next day.'

I listened to my uncle and reflected on his theory about the fat man's happiness. I found that my uncle wasn't wrong. It was his deep life experience and the age difference between us. I hadn't encountered anyone from my background who possessed such depth and wisdom. My father had no wisdom, and my maternal uncle wasn't convincing either. Perhaps the limping man was intelligent and kind, with his unique way of life, but we didn't spend enough time together for me to form a complete picture of him. Only his beautiful memory remains in my mind, which is the same image my uncle has of him he recalls him from time to time.

When I told my uncle about the discovery of the fat man's thefts and my hesitation in informing him. I also mentioned the conversation between us and the fat man's commitment afterward.

My uncle looked at me with a half-smile, stroking his small white beard, and said:

'And did he tell you how many people he killed before he came here?'

I was shocked to learn that my uncle knew about the killing that took place that distant evening on the roof of the shop. He knew a great deal about the fat man's life. He told me:

'To build a successful business, you need to understand the people around you. I mean, you need to understand their past well. The past itself isn't necessary, but it shapes our present. We need to understand it to control the present moment with our positive traits and to overcome the weaknesses that reside in us as humans. No one is born perfect.'

The question that came to my mind was, does the fat man know that the master is aware that he is robbing him and does not care about it just as the fat man knows perfectly well that my uncle is certain that he does not show any interest in women.

I didn't seek an immediate answer because I had learned to stay calm. The slow fire that cooks the meat is the same fuel that drives a person's life. Let things slowly sink in over time to reach their distant goals. This last piece of wisdom is my own; I didn't hear it from my uncle.

On the day I followed my aunt home, she asked me to stay with her for a while. She wanted me by her side, not for any particular reason, but because she was reminiscing about her son, who had been killed by mercenaries who came by planes from faraway neighbouring countries. They entered at night and destroyed everything—communication systems, the local radio station, and they took over the national television. They killed innocent citizens, leaving their intended targets unharmed.

My aunt recounted the events to me while crying. She opened a closet in the house that seemed to have been closed for years. She brought out her son's clothes, shoes, books, and toys, which included colourful balls and models of famous buildings like the Eiffel Tower, the Egyptian pyramids, Greenwich Clock in London, the newly built mosque in the capital called the Mosque of the Two Niles. Each toy had a story, and she narrated them all. He also had beautifully written, colourful school notebooks. I spent half the night with her until my uncle came home, and I asked to leave, though she wanted me to stay and spend with her, in her arms that night.

My life continued with work and this family, which became a support for me, away from the past. I felt great joy and love for life. There was no time for rest, just work. The shop was always crowded with customers. Days and nights passed as I deepened my knowledge and experience.

One evening, after finishing work, my friend the shoeshiner stood before me in the shop. I was wearing the white shawarma master's apron, which had become part of my appearance along with my limp. For a moment, my vision blurred, and then I saw clearly seconds later. That was my friend.

His gaze told me he was angry, at least unhappy about my absence from our residence for several days. To be realistic, it had been weeks since we renovated the shop and carried out the maintenance. I had nothing to say or apologise for. I knew I had failures in life, one of them being my neglect of friends, as my uncle once said.

My friend grabbed my apron violently, then smiled and said:

'I didn't come to quarrel. I came to say goodbye; I'm leaving.'

I could see many things in his eyes, things that remained unspoken. He simply expressed them by hugging me tightly, once, twice, and then said:

'The war has reignited in the land of our ancestors. They need more fighters there. I don't know if I'll return.'

We walked together until we reached the main street, then the familiar alley and the room behind it. He had packed his papers and paintings into a new suitcase that he seemed to have bought recently; I hadn't seen it before. The place was dimly lit.

He told me that a new building was being constructed on the other corner of the street, and for several days, the electricity had been cut off in the room because of it as if it were a sign that we wouldn't stay here.

He handed me the bag and entrusted me with keeping it safe if he returned, I was to give it back, and if not, it would serve as a memory of a wonderful time in his life.

We both said goodbye to the room after we moved the necessary belongings to my room at the shop. My friend spent that night with me before leaving for the south the next morning.

Since that day, I haven't had a specific friend. Work became my only friend, along with the family that loved me, and the fat man with whom I spent time engaged in constant activity.

Since I had mastered many tasks, I was increasingly given the responsibility to do them instead of him. I didn't think he was shirking his duties; rather, he was giving me the space to develop my skills.

During siesta hours, we continued to pray together and lie down for a while in the back room. At night, the fat man would leave.

To this day, I don't know exactly where he lived, nor did I ever ask until one night, he was troubled. This state started with him in the morning, and he even made several mistakes at work. I managed to rectify these with the customers by stepping in quickly. For example, he would put red peppers in some customers' orders without their request, or the opposite would happen—he wouldn't heat the bread properly, or he wouldn't wrap the sandwiches as he should. I realised that something was troubling him, as I had never seen him act like this before.

That night, after the day had passed with all its mistakes, he asked if he could stay in my room and informed me that he couldn't return to his place. There was something he couldn't talk about, and I didn't object; I let him stay with me.

I set up a mattress on the floor for him. I only had one bed. He slept like a dead man until he woke up after about two hours. I was still awake, reading a book about developing human skills in time management.

Those days, I had returned to reading, something I had started in the room with my friend who had travelled. I had a modest library with a few books I bought from a used book market near the church. I went there once and brought them all with me. All the books were about work, success, and self-development. My uncle was happy that I was doing this, although he remarked that practical experience was better than searching for the secrets of life among the pages of books, but he conceded that everyone has their own way of learning.

The fat man got up and told me he could now leave, but he asked me to walk him there for some reason. He didn't explain, and he didn't agree to my insistence that he stay with me until morning. He just insisted that I walk with him. So we walked together.

He seemed like someone who was afraid of something, but he didn't reveal his fears to me. He kept looking around as we walked down the street until we had covered a distance of at least two kilometres.

We reached a ground-floor house with a small door. That door led to a room with a bathroom separate from the main house. This is where the fat man lived. I wanted to say goodbye and return, but he begged me to stay with him and he explained the reason for his anxieties the day before:

'I received word that my brothers would be arriving here today. I don't know when exactly they will arrive. That's why I'm afraid.'

I asked him:

'But what are you afraid of?'

My question was meaningless. I wanted to understand the reason for his sense of apprehension. He continued to explain:

'At first, I decided to escape by staying with you all night, but then I finally decided to come back here to face them whenever they arrived…'

He fell silent for a while. He was breathing heavily like a slaughtered bull. He lay down on the wooden bed, his large body causing the wood to creak.

He reached under the bed and took out a bottle of wine, half full. He took several quick sips, with barely any time between them. His eyes turned red, and his face grew pale in the dim light of the room. He said to me:

'I'm very scared… Come, let me hold you so I can dispel my fears.'

He slowly reached out toward me. The alcohol had quickly taken hold of him. I thought to myself, was this all a ploy on his part in his mix of reality and imagination to bring me here?

I heard him repeat what he had said, mumbling:

'I will heal if I find a warm embrace… I am lost and tormented in this world… I am alone… I am mad…'

He couldn't move. His body was too heavy. His pale face gradually faded, and the smell of alcohol filled the room. I turned on the fan at medium speed, turned off the light, and let him sink into sleep.

I returned to my room at the shop to spend the rest of the night until early dawn, when I woke up to receive the meat and vegetable suppliers who came from farms on the outskirts of the big city. They unloaded the goods from the small truck, and I arranged them in their places in the fridge and on the shelves before making myself a cup of hot tea.

Shawarma

I sat on the plastic chair that my uncle would sit on all day at the entrance of the shop watching the street. A few passersby were out in the early morning, and there were drops of rain drizzling on the street. I could also see a plane landing at the airport, imagining myself as one of its passengers.

The fat man appeared at the beginning of the alley near the street that connected to the shop. I saw him approaching as if he hadn't left the state he was in.

He greeted me mechanically and entered the shop, where he began his routine work but he seemed to be in a worse mood than yesterday. I suggested he sit in the back room or rest for a while and that I would continue working alone until he felt capable of performing well.

He followed my advice... entered... After about fifteen minutes, I checked on him; he had fallen asleep again, like that slaughtered bull.

My uncle arrived around seven, just as the rain was intensifying. He was carrying an umbrella, anticipating the sudden change in weather, as this was not the season for rain.

He asked me about the fat man and why he was late, as it wasn't like him to be absent.

I told him he was inside and explained what had happened, that he had been troubled by something since yesterday that I couldn't quite understand. My uncle became concerned as he listened to me. He asked:

'Does he have a fever or some illness?'

'No... He's scared of something I can't pinpoint... and he won't talk about it.'

I didn't tell him in detail what had happened the night before. I just told him that I had walked him to his place.

My uncle entered the back room and stayed there for some time before coming out silently. He was clearly sad. He said to me:

'He's never experienced something like this; I've known him for many years. No matter how scared he was, he always remains happy, at least feels a little sad or scares. But he never loses his love for life. He loves himself very much and loves being a part of the world.'

I waited for my uncle to finish, then asked him:

'Did he tell you anything? Or explain the reason for his fears?'

'No... He didn't say anything. He's distressed and irritable... Let's leave him until he calms down.'

Around noon the sun was pouring its rays onto the earth again, the rain had stopped, the sky had cleared, and the early morning breeze had dissipated.

A large truck (lorry) stopped in front of the shop, and a group of men jumped down from its load. They didn't speak to anyone. Their faces were grim, suggesting something ominous surrounded them. It was as if they had come from a catastrophe. Two of them entered the shop quickly, shouting:

'Where is he? We won't let him go!'

My uncle watched the situation without intervening, while the customers observed what was happening. They saw the sharp tools the men were carrying, large knives and cleavers. One of them shouted loudly:

'Search the place thoroughly... Make sure he's not here.'

Another shouted:

'If he's not in the house, he must have come here.'

It was only a matter of minutes before they stormed the back part of the shop and everyone heard the sounds of a fierce fight... curses, blows, shouts, and clashes. Then we saw a man being thrown through the door that separated the interior from the front, as the fat man had flung him far away, followed by another. He was holding one of the cleavers in his hand. He had struck one of the men at his face with it.

Moments later, blood started pouring from the man's face that split open by the cleaver. Blood had spilled onto the shop floor.

It was a very bad day, a horrible day that brought misfortune. I felt that way from what I was witnessing, unable to comprehend what was happening before me. My uncle, too, was extremely upset by what was unfolding in front of him.

Three police officers had arrived at the shop, carrying their rifles, surrounding the men—there were four, excluding the one who had died. They chained them with strong chains and also handcuffed the fat man.

He was casting glances at me and my uncle, with a sadness evident on his face. He looked at us intensely, as if he wanted to apologise for some secret in his life that he could He not share with us, for some unknown and mysterious reason.

The large truck had moved, driven by a police officer, and onions scattered and bounced around like balls, spilling out of the bags loaded onto it. The sign on the truck indicated that it had come from a distant place outside the capital.

After this incident, the shop remained closed for two weeks by police order because the restaurant had become a crime scene, as defined by the detective who visited several times.

I was not allowed to stay at the shop during the specified period, so my uncle insisted that I stay with them at the house in the room where I had slept that night. I felt that my aunt was not entirely pleased with my staying at their house. This was not her initial stance—she had welcomed me at first, but her attitude changed after I overheard her talking to a woman dressed in a blue gown and large copper earrings that dangled from her ears. This woman visited her during the day when my uncle was away at the police station, where he was summoned almost daily.

From what I observed, the woman seemed to be a fortune-teller, casting seashells on the ground to predict the future and determine one's fate.

My aunt tried to conceal this, but my old experiences in the town made it easy to discover. My uncle himself sensed that something was happening behind his back and asked me in the afternoon:

'Did anyone visit your aunt?'

I didn't lie to him; I had never told him anything untrue. I told him what I saw and my exact suspicion. He replied:

'I figured as much, I just wanted to be sure. I know she has a deep belief in these things… She's spent a lot of money on them… It's her only weakness.'

The next day, the fortune-teller came again. My aunt closed all the doors and windows of the inner house, and I smelled the scent of incense wafting from inside, accompanied by the sound of chanting that seemed to come and go as if it were echoing from the depths of a well.

I imagined my uncle arriving and discovering the situation, but my imagination was wrong. A few minutes later, I heard a voice calling me—it was the strange woman's voice, asking me to come at my aunt's request.

I entered the room where they were. My aunt was sitting on the floor in front of the fortune-teller, who had spread sand on the tiles and was tossing shells onto it, muttering incomprehensible words.

I looked at my aunt, who today appeared older than I knew her to be. She was only about five years younger than my uncle, but today she seemed much older than him. I don't know why; perhaps it was just my imagination.

The fortune-teller pointed towards me and said:

'Keep him away; he will bring no good.'

She spoke in front of me, completely unconcerned about my presence.

I saw my aunt's face turn grim as she stared into my eyes. I didn't feel the warmth she used to show when she spoke to me as if I were her son. The fortune-teller's broad face was unsettling, and I felt as if she harboured ill intentions.

My aunt took out a bundle of money from a small bag and handed it to the woman, who counted it eagerly, wetting her fingertips with saliva and repeatedly counting with anticipation, before sipping the rest of the Turkish coffee in front of her in the same way the limping man would slurp juices.

She tossed the cup onto the sand indifferently and stood up to leave, while my aunt remained sitting on the floor, deep in thought on a matter. I imagined she would immediately throw me out of her house, but that didn't happen.

Fearing that the atmosphere would become tense, I chose to go out for a walk in the city and thought about visiting some old friends in what they called the 'European Street'.

On my way, my uncle saw me, so I returned to the house with him. As we walked back, I told him exactly what had happened that day, as he had made me promise to tell him everything. He had told me:

'Your aunt has been on edge since our son left. She finds some solace in you and often tells me so. She even wishes you could stay with us at the house always… But these days, she's anxious because of what happened at the shop. She's become a pessimist of strangers, as she tells me… But you're not a stranger, my son'

I interrupted my uncle, which I rarely did, as I usually never cut him off:

'Uncle, if my presence bothers you, I will find a place to stay until the shop reopens and I can return to my room there'

He held me close—something he rarely did, unlike my aunt. He kissed me several times on my cheek, making me feel the fatherly warmth I had never experienced in my life. He said:

'My son, don't say that. I trust you completely... and so does your aunt. She's just tense, that's all... You'll see, with time, that she loves you more than you think and that she'll never abandon you.'

My uncle's words instilled in me the conviction to wait and not rush into leaving their house. I avoided speaking to my aunt or being around her, and my uncle was also careful about this.

Several days passed during which she didn't see me as I stayed out of the house most of the time, until the two weeks were over, and the shop reopened. I returned to my room. The very next day, my aunt arrived in the afternoon. She hurried through the customers to hug me and kiss me, asking with reproach:

'Where have you been hiding, my son, all these days?'

I replied with a white lie:

'Forgive me, Aunt, I was busy sorting things out at the shop.'

We had lost some items, like the back glass of the large shawarma stand, behind which the chef stands, as a large part of it had shattered. Cleaning the tiles had also been exhausting, especially as the smell of blood took a long time and a lot of chemicals to eliminate completely. But that was not the real reason for not seeing my aunt, and she knew it very well. She looked at me and smiled in her usual way at me, saying:

'Your uncle is travelling this afternoon... and you will come to stay with me at the house.'

She left, gesturing for me not to be late. The day dragged on with the routine of daily life. I was alone, and I had to prove to myself that I was capable and challenge myself. I can't evaluate it now; days will pass before I fully understand whether I am truly capable of facing a real challenge or not.

5
In my Turkish uncle's house

My uncle was summoned to court multiple times. The days following the fat man's imprisonment and trial were harsh and surrounded by sorrow, even though the man proved to us— not just in our imagination— that he was a killer. In the past, one might think that his oral tales contained some fantasy or were entirely made up, but this recent experience complicated matters.

I heard my uncle calling me after we reached the large court gate, asking me to sit in the last row of the hall filled with rows of wooden benches. The place was buzzing with people until the man, for whom everyone stood up, entered and tapped a pointed wooden piece on the table. The scene felt like a classroom.

The fat man stood behind an iron cage, silent. He had lost a little weight and glanced at me from afar with kind eyes. I was pained by his sight, and tears welled up in my eyes. I couldn't resist the weakness that overcame me, and I began to recall repeated and beautiful moments we had together, making me realize at that moment that I loved this man despite everything.

As my uncle says, our weaknesses are many, and we should seek out the positive things. I waved my hand, and he raised his in return. He seemed unconcerned with what was happening, as if he lived in another world outside this crowded courtroom, filled mostly with his relatives who had come from various cities across the country—his relatives and those of the deceased, no difference, for the deceased was his brother. Cain killed Abel. Such are the sons of Adam.

A man wearing a loose black robe, tightly secured glasses with a long chain hanging on both sides with dark lenses began reading several documents. He continued reading for more than half an hour, occasionally interrupted by the judge.

I didn't care about what I heard; I was thinking about the fat man's fate. I overheard some whispering that he would likely face execution. These whisperers were his family and loved ones who seemed to have all turned against him. No one here looked at him with pity; their faces were grim and unkind. I felt a hatred towards them. The fat man could have been among the dead; they were the ones who attacked him and wanted to kill him. So what's the difference? There must be a mistake in the law.

The judge called my uncle. He stood up and was asked several questions, but I only focused on the end:

'He has worked with me for many years… Yes, I have never seen him make a mistake.'

The judge concluded my uncle's testimony, and the session was adjourned, with the verdict to be announced in two weeks.

We left without speaking to each other. This time, I couldn't bear to watch the fat man being dragged with shackles on his hands and feet as he was loaded into a hideous black van without windows. They opened the back gate, tossed him inside like a rat, and closed it. He was silent and brave, showing no sign of fear.

As I was observing what was happening to the fat man, my uncle stood talking with the man in the loose black robe about the trial. I heard the man say to my uncle:

'I tried my best to save him, but it's very difficult for him to be acquitted.'

My uncle took out a bundle of money from his trouser pocket and handed it to the man, who quickly counted it without paying attention to the people around. His demeanour was striking, and I sensed that my uncle was uncomfortable with the scene, especially since I knew how much he despised those who flaunted money publicly.

We returned home, where my aunt was waiting for us. She looked very radiant today, fully dressed up as if she were preparing to attend an event. Her hair was washed and styled, and her face glowed like that of a child. My uncle was aware of where she was going but didn't know she intended to take me with her. That's why I had to go with my uncle to the European market.

We took a taxi and bought a full suit for me. That evening, I looked like a little prince, almost identical to their son, who they lost to mercenaries.

My aunt was very happy and shed tears as we entered a hall in one of the city's large clubs. I had never entered such a place before. I had only passed by it while wandering the streets, observing the appearance and clothing of the people who came here. Now, I was one of them.

As much as I felt proud and elated, I was somewhat sad that my mother couldn't see me in this wonderful suit. As usual, I forgot and lived a memorable moment in my life.

I was warmly received; elderly women kissed my cheeks and smelled the expensive perfume that my uncle bought for me on my aunt's recommendation, who had made a list of what needed to be brought for this night. It was a grand wedding for one of the city's notable sons, and I didn't care who the bride or groom was.

I was contemplating life in another place, a place I hadn't discovered before. I remembered that my maternal uncle and his wife used to go out in full splendour at night to such events, but they never took me to any of them. And I wouldn't have remembered my uncle if I hadn't noticed him sitting with his wife at one of the tables, with a girl beside them, whom I think was my cousin who had returned from outside the country.

I wondered whether they would recognised me and if anything unfortunate would happen. I thought about whether I should tell my aunt or try to ignore them. And if they recognised me, would they care? I wasn't sure.

The place was bustling with people of different colours, shapes, and appearances, under dazzling lights. It was the unknown half of that city. Here was the real life you don't see on the street. From that day, I began to discover a new life and another world that I might find myself a part of over time, in my own way.

The food was served; it was a cocktail of dishes on elegant paper plates. Boys my age were serving the guests, likely from a company. I compared the weddings in the village with this one—there was no comparison. And as I was lost in thoughts between yesterday and today, the singer's voice rose. It was that famous artist known as Africa's first singer.

The musicians were on a high platform, dressed in uniform, and the music harmonized with the bursts of colourful shapes that began to fill the sky. A man was launching something into the sky, filling the horizon with a flood of colourful lights.

Amidst the waves of guests dancing to the music's rhythm, my maternal uncle noticed me near my Turkish aunt. He glanced at me once and then again. His wife wasn't paying attention, while his daughter was dancing with a man older than her. There was no need for proof.

The central area covered with a carpet was crowded with dancers. The smell of alcohol filled the place and that strange scent I had smelled before at the limping man and my uncle's wife.

Cigarette smoke rose, blocking the horizon. Most of the people here had turned into ghostly figures swaying in front of me, as my vision became distorted due to the randomly falling light.

The lady sensed that I might be a little upset, so she reassured me that we would leave soon. She was unlike the majority, sitting in her seat without participating in the dancing, merely exchanging bright smiles with anyone who looked her way and greeted her.

Minutes later, my uncle stood before us and greeted my aunt. She didn't show much interest in him. I don't think she knew him. While she reflected positive emotions in her facial features and returned his greetings, even standing up for him, she also displayed unmistakable surprise at shaking his hand.

He extended his hand toward me, and I extended mine without much care or regard for the fact that I was the one he knew well—his nephew. I pretended to be someone else and pulled my hand back politely, unmoved, before my aunt sat down.

My uncle appeared bewildered by my behaviour, unsure if I was really who he thought I was, for my elegance and appearance didn't match the old boy he knew. I didn't know what my feelings were, but I couldn't find a way to pass even a shred of love toward him at that moment. For some reason, I felt contempt for him without thinking a lot the reasons.

He was about to open his mouth to speak, to ask, and finally said:

'Where have you been, boy?'

My aunt's face changed. She looked at my uncle with clear annoyance, as if telling him to respect himself, for the word 'boy' was provocative to her, although the word was lovely for me and her when she called me using it.

She indicated her desire to end the conversation with a stranger by pointing to me to sit and saying:

'What is it, sir? Why are you addressing my son in this manner?'

My uncle stepped back, visibly puzzled, caught between disbelief and belief. His face was suddenly flushed with sweat that flowed from the cheeks and the wide forehead. He took a puff from his pipe as he walked, oblivious to his surroundings, almost falling to the ground after colliding with a family's table. I didn't know whether to laugh or just thank my aunt for making me her son. I remained silent, feeling no guilt.

On the way back, my aunt asked me:

'Who was that man? Is he one of the shop's customers?'

Then she added:

'His behaviour in speaking was quite impolite.'

I replied without hesitation:

'He's my maternal uncle.'

She was astonished and said:

'So, he recognised you.'

I responded bravely:

'I don't care if he recognised me or not.'

She didn't ask further and never brought up the topic again, whether that night or later. It passed as if it were a dream. However, my uncle's defeated image stayed in my mind. I sometimes felt sympathy for him, only to quickly push it aside to continue with my usual life, as yesterday didn't matter.

The days passed, and I had almost no friends left after my friend travelled to the south, and I stopped hearing from him. I had lost track of the war news since I left my street companions, as work consumed most of my time. It became my definite world, and my uncle and aunt started to care for me.

I moved in with them, and they prepared the room where I had once slept, hanging my picture next to the picture of a woman I learned was my uncle's mother, who had passed away years ago.

Life was mostly peaceful, except for occasional memories of the past. But a restless seed within me strongly prevented me from looking back or thinking about my hometown and family. It was something I couldn't control, perhaps an illness according to the psychiatrist who once tested street kids.

After the fat man left the shop, I was left alone, handling everything by myself. My uncle wanted to hire another worker, but I insisted on managing it on my own, as long as the workload remained manageable. If the business grew, we could hire dozens of workers in the future, a vision I saw clearly in my mind.

As for the fat man, he remained in prison after the judge sentenced him to 20 years on that unforgettable day. I thought about how he would be almost 80 by the time he was released, while I would be around 40—if we both lived that long. Life feels brutal when you face it by counting years and ages.

As we left the courthouse, my uncle said:

'The lawyer did everything he could, but it didn't work.'

'Would his siblings' forgiveness have freed him?' I asked.

'They refused, and forgiveness wouldn't matter as long as the sentence wasn't death. He didn't kill intentionally'

Another question came to me suddenly:

'Uncle, you once told me something... did he ever tell you how many people he killed before coming here? Did you know he was a killer? How many people did he kill?'

My uncle smiled and replied:

'It's mostly an exaggeration. He told a story, but I don't know how true it is. Even if he killed someone, it wasn't intentional.'

Life went on, and with time, we forgot about the fat man. His memory faded from my mind, and my uncle no longer mentioned him. But I still recall that painful farewell when I saw my uncle's tears falling. He was genuinely sad, murmuring about how companionship never fades away.

On that day, I saw a new side of my uncle—a heart full of love for those loyal to him, for those who truly loved him. There was no doubt the fat man loved my uncle and was loyal to him. He did his duty seriously, and any small flaws meant little compared to his brighter side.

I became known as the Turkish man's son. Many thought I was truly his son, and I never denied or confirmed it. My theory was to let people say what they wanted, which was the same belief my uncle had. Where else would I have gotten it but from him? He had become my father and teacher; he and my aunt became my entire world. They showed me nothing but overflowing love.

My aunt once suggested I return to school to continue my education, but I no longer wanted that. I found myself in the world of the market, the shop, and shawarma. Schools no longer meant anything to me. I saw hundreds, if not thousands, graduating every year with no jobs. Some of them even came to our shop looking for work. It's not about the value of education itself, my son, but something mysterious called fate or human will.

Let me simplify it for you. In life, we often rush in different directions and take various paths, but there's something mysterious that controls us, guiding us toward our destiny, crafted for us by divine care, It is the fate woven for us in the exciting unknown, which never errs. People try to become many things but end up being just one thing—that's all. This is who I am, my son.

My uncle never interfered in my decisions. He only filled me with wisdom and virtues that could help me, but the decision was always mine. Even in matters of work, that was his approach. He would say that intelligence isn't crafted by schools but is often diminished by them. Perhaps he was speaking from his own experience, though I never knew much about it or asked him. He was saying that and many other things, and I had to make a decision.

Over time, my aunt gave up insisting that I become a doctor or engineer, or any other prestigious profession, as people say. There's a belief that to make money, you must pursue one of those careers. One day, she said to me:

'Look at your father; what does he lack? He didn't stay in school for long.'

She started calling him my father, and I became the son, and she was my mother. This was my family. There's no escape; it's fate. Some parts of it are wonderful, and others are harsh.

The years passed quickly, racing each other. Sometimes, a person doesn't even feel the passage of time as it speeds by, and sometimes it slows down, hitting difficult and rough patches.

Over the years, I grew into a man, reaching about twenty years old. I had a small moustache, a clean-shaven face, and I was dedicated to hard work. By this time, I had developed my own way of living.

There were moments when I felt a deep sorrow or a sharp sting, like needles piercing my body. It was the longing for my family.

Over time, I resisted this feeling and eventually overcame it completely, to the point where I saw the distant town and my family as nothing more than faint, old ghosts in my life.

My mother's image grew more distant, especially as my vision became blurred, prompting me to use glasses to correct my sight. With the glasses, things appeared clearer and closer, except for the past, which continued to drift further away.

My uncle, as usual, was away on one of his trips, probably attending to some business in his homeland, Turkey. I didn't usually ask about things unless they were explicitly told to me, and later I found out that he had a daughter there, possibly about ten years older than me. She might be around thirty or more—I wasn't exactly sure. She was from his first wife, who passed away in Istanbul from a horrible disease over twenty years ago.

Since his daughter was married and lived with her husband, she, as my aunt mentioned, focused on her own life. She had never visited here, as her world was based in Turkey. She worked in journalism as I knew and also wrote books, stories, and novels.

I asked my aunt:

'Have you two met before?'

'Yes, but it was a long time ago, my dear,' she replied.

My uncle loved his daughter, and he loved me too, especially as I grew older, reminding him more and more of his late son. Every year as I grew, he would pat me on the shoulder and often say:

'You're growing, my boy.'

I imagined that he saw his son in me or perhaps had come to believe that I was him. People sometimes invent illusions and come to believe them, finding it hard to return to reality. Maybe I was part of that illusion for this family. However, illusions can't turn into the overwhelming love that my aunt showed me. She carefully supervised my affairs, was deeply involved in my life, and discussed my situation with my uncle.

There was no clear sign that would reflect the reality of my situation or oppose the affection they showered upon me. I couldn't imagine living a better life elsewhere, for the kind feelings people express are what make a person happy and passionately in love with life and ambition.

In my uncle's private room, where I had initially felt shy about entering, two pictures were hanging: one of his late wife and one of his daughter. Over the years, the whole house became my domain, and I could enter anywhere without feeling awkward.

In the picture, the late wife appeared beautiful and young. I learned she had passed away in the prime of her youth, before reaching twenty-five. She gave birth to her daughter, and two or three years later, her fate was sealed by that dreaded disease.

The daughter remained with her maternal family in Istanbul, who raised her until she grew up and got married. The daughter bore a striking resemblance to me, especially the sorrowful expression on her face, something that would be noticeable to anyone who looked closely. I figured she must think a lot, given that she was a writer.

My uncle mentioned that writing was exhausting, based on his daughter's experience. Yet he also said that it was a grand human endeavour, especially when the writer is dedicated to their craft and fights to make the world a better place, deserving of respect and trust in the future.

I didn't know how people wrote books; I was only interested in reading. As I told you, I focused on books that developed my skills in life and work. I once saw my uncle carrying a book written by his daughter in Turkish, a language I knew nothing about. Sure, I had memorized a few phrases or words from my uncle and aunt, but reading or writing Turkish was out of the question—until the day I decided to educate myself in that area.

I made a plan with my aunt, whom I would later discover was well-educated and intelligent, even without reading books. Gradually, over six months, we would stay up late at night, and I would wake up for work at dawn. By then, I had started to decode reading and speaking. This allowed me to read, at first, the titles of my cousin's books and some lines here and there. I even browsed through Turkish newspapers that my uncle brought back from Istanbul during his visits—he went there at least twice a year.

Over time, everything was going well, especially since I had a knack for quickly learning things I was interested in, and mastering them thoroughly.

Learning Turkish was just one of many interests that piqued my curiosity at certain times, sparking a desire to understand or learn something new. This was part of my approach to life. Besides being occupied with work, I often sought hobbies or enjoyable activities to fill my time, ensuring I wouldn't become stagnant or lose my connection to life's routine. My uncle used to say:

'A person rusts over time if they have no interests outside of work.'

As I learned Turkish, I had access to several of my cousin's books. But to be honest, it took me a long time to actually read them. It wasn't because my language skills were lacking—far from it. My attention had simply shifted to other things. Still, I was keen to understand my uncle's life through what his daughter had written.

He had told me there were subtle hints, even if not direct, in her writings, and that my homeland was mentioned as a place where someone sought refuge, in which a person searching for himself and his future found a real support upon which they could leave behind the pain of the past. He said this without ever revealing the nature or extent of that pain.

The direct reason for my preoccupation was that one day, after I turned twenty-one, my aunt (my mother) surprised me by telling me a secret, urging me to keep it to myself. She explained that this secret would motivate me to work harder and focus better on my responsibilities at the shop.

She told me that my uncle had allocated a portion of his wealth for me in a legal document filed in court, which would only be revealed when the time was right. She gently requested:

'I know you're serious and discreet. Promise me you won't let anyone know I told you.'

A thought crossed my mind, and I asked her:

'But doesn't he have a daughter who's more entitled than me?'

'She doesn't need anything. Besides, this arrangement was made at my request. You're my son, aren't you?' she replied.

I didn't know how to respond. She hugged me, gazing into the distance, lost in thought. I didn't know what she was thinking about when my uncle walked in. He saw me in her embrace, smiled without disturbing us, and quietly made his way to his private room. That room, I imagined, was where he liked to sit and reflect on his past—his memories, childhood, and maybe his old life's journey.

I once mentioned this to him, and he said:

'You and she are no different. Both of you are fond of creating stories and imagining things.'

He meant his daughter, and I understood that. He added:

'I prefer imagination that is applied in reality, in work and livelihood.'

My aunt's secret remained a secret, and I was never sure if my uncle suspected that I knew. But I don't think so, because my relationship with the work continued to grow and develop. Within a few months of learning the secret, I had introduced important innovations to the shop that supported marketing and increased customer traffic.

My uncle had never paid much attention to advertising, which was precisely where I stepped in. I made a deal with a local company to place fixed ads around the city. One of them was at the airport, near its main entrance. We paid some money, but the return was better. My uncle didn't oppose my ideas, even though he had never tried them before.

As a result, customers started coming directly from the airport to our shop, which had also undergone improvements. We installed a large shawarma statue in the small square outside, which lit up at night, glowing brightly and drawing attention. Its lights would trigger the appetites of passersby, as I overheard some of them say, 'You can't walk by without feeling your stomach rumble.'

These advertisements and innovations, as I called them, despite bringing prosperity in a short period and reinforcing my uncle's confidence in my abilities, and perhaps he felt that his decision, which he did not tell me about, was successful, but as the same time these changes brought some temporary troubles. But generally, a person learns from their experiences and tries to turn every problem into something positive instead of dwelling on regret. This is almost what happened.

Within days of the shop's growth and the noticeable increase in customers, unfamiliar faces began to appear. A man would arrive in a small car, park not far from the shop, and quickly order a sandwich. While eating, he would study the customers, counting them and recording numbers in a large notebook with a thick pen. He would then pay and leave. After two days, there were two men, then three. One day, a very tall man accompanied them, carrying an even larger notebook. He stood next to my uncle, speaking to him, though I couldn't hear what was being said from a distance. However, I could see that my uncle was visibly upset, saying aloud:

'This has never happened before. What's changed?'

The very tall man was furious, speaking rudely, while the customers stopped eating to watch. I, too, stopped carving meat in front of the fire, observing the situation as it escalated into a one-sided argument. I knew my uncle's patience and tolerance for abuse, but I couldn't bear hearing the vile insults directed at him or seeing distress on him while he was silent—being called a foreign donkey, a thief, a Turkish son of a… and other slurs.

I understood their intent: they were trying to say that the shop was lacking legal procedures, even though I knew for sure that everything was in order, following all regulations, and health and safety standards were strictly adhered to. My uncle never overlooked anything, and he renewed the shop's license annually. Weeks ahead of time he ensured the decoration was refreshed and all aspects of cleanliness and service were prepared. I had supervised all of this alongside my uncle. So there was something unclear, ambiguous or intentional about this shameful intervention.

Just as I was about to intervene because I became too angry, one of the regular customers, distinguished by his attire and who seemed like a respectable man—if not the opposite—stepped in.

My experience in these matters had sharpened over the years, and I no longer judged people at first glance. I could discern characters and read faces of people from their general appearance.

This customer motioned toward the very tall man to step aside. At first, the tall man ignored him, but after the other men whispered in his ear, he reluctantly moved aside to listen to the well-dressed man respectfully. After a brief conversation, the rude men gathered their things and left, never to be seen again.

The customers resumed their meals while the well-dressed man exchanged a few words with my uncle before leaving too.

'It's not true what they claim, that the law has changed and a foreigner can't own a shop.'

He paused briefly and added:

'I know exactly what they're after. Let me apologise, sir, for what had happened.'

Neither my uncle nor I knew who this man was. He left without introducing himself, and my uncle later told me he was too embarrassed to ask. Some of the customers had also been watching the man with great curiosity, but no one could say they knew who he was.

This incident reminded me of the day my old friend came and got me out of prison—or the detention center—an unsolved mystery that lingers in my mind to this day. Such things have happened to me throughout my life. I ponder them for a while, but eventually, I forget or pretend to forget, because life, as always, moves forward, presenting new events that force a shift in focus in another something.

The meaning is that sometimes we understand, and sometimes we don't. Only when we meet our end will we grasp how some details of our existence formed? Yet, many mysteries will remain entirely inexplicable. However, the secret behind this particular incident was revealed just a few days later.

Another day had arrived, and I was dressed as dazzling as my uncle, preparing for a professional photographer to capture the storefront. We had found this photographer through a customer, who described him as dedicated, precise, and delivering impressive results, all for a reasonable price—rare qualities in this country, where many claim expertise.

The man arrived, camera in hand, and set it up at what seemed like a distant corner of the street. As I accompanied him, he explained to me:

'Photography is an art, my boy. The angle must be carefully chosen.'

He appeared youthful, despite clear signs of aging. He wore an unbuttoned jacket; with tools I couldn't fully identify in the large right pocket—one of them being a magnifying glass that he held behind the camera. He repeatedly looked through it, glancing at the scene before adjusting the tripod, and moving it to a new position.

After capturing dozens of shots to later select from for the newspaper ad I had planned—in one of my promotional ideas that had pleased my uncle—a woman approached us. She stepped out of a four-wheel drive, driven by a bald chauffeur. She wore a sheer white dress, revealing much of her body without care for those around.

She paused in front of the shop, glanced at the sign, and then asked me:

'Where's Mr. Turkish?'

I pointed inside:

'He's in there'

With a surprising lightness for her somewhat full figure and average height, she entered the shop and spoke with my uncle. I didn't eavesdrop, keeping my usual distance. When she left, my uncle called me over, watching my face for a reaction.

'She's the wife of a prominent politician, and she's here to make an offer to buy the shop for a very generous price. What do you think?'

'Buy…?'

'Yes, and she wants you to stay on because you know the craft. She's well-informed about everything happening here.'

'Do you know who her husband is?'

'I don't know him personally, only that he's her husband. She's also a friend of your aunt.'

Of course, my uncle wouldn't sell the shop—the harvest of his life's work, now just beginning to bear fruit after a long journey of patience. And I, not being an owner, but I wouldn't want the sale either. It wasn't about inheriting a portion of the wealth, as my aunt often suggested.

I was thinking that this place had become part of my world, including my uncle. Even if someone else bought it, I couldn't enjoy the same freedom working for them as I do now. Besides, I was preoccupied with the thought that this was our family legacy, one I would never allow to be squandered. As curious as I was about the politician's identity, my focus was on preventing any idea of selling the shop.

The politician's wife had arranged with my uncle to return later that night, close to midnight, to get his answer. She claimed urgency. The meeting would be at our house, and we waited. My uncle had made up his mind—no, absolutely not—but he planned to handle it politely:

'These powerful people shouldn't be opposed openly. They can become vicious when they want something.'

The woman arrived, and my aunt welcomed her warmly. They knew each other well and exchanged kisses on the cheek. They chatted, sipping Turkish coffee. It was late, but the powerful families were known to love staying up late; I'd seen it at my uncle's house for years. They were night lovers.

The evening ended with the woman receiving her answer: no. It came from my aunt, skilfully delivered:

'No one would willingly cut off their hand and hand it to someone else.'

The politician's wife's expression changed—she didn't seem angry but tried to appear composed. I knew their type well. They display silence and poise, only to transform later into beasts that devour everything in their path.

In truth, I was terrified of what tomorrow might bring. My uncle was also uneasy. We stayed up until nearly dawn, speaking little. I thought about my future—just when I had made significant strides toward a better life, disaster loomed. I couldn't trust anyone else.

My uncle, too, was worried, more than I had ever seen him. After a long silence, he said:

'This country is sinking into the abyss, my boy. I don't think I'll stay much longer if things keep going this way. We'll go back to Turkey, and you'll come with us.'

He was referring to how much had changed in the last two decades. In recent years, a class of merchants had taken over the country's affairs—politicians masquerading as businessmen. They had failed to save the country from ongoing disasters, wars ravaging the south, and famines in the east and west, so they turned to their personal desires. Perhaps this had been their intention from the start.

My uncle was deeply frustrated by the situation, though he had never been interested in politics before. He had always been focused on his work and nothing else:

'But the flood has reached our doorstep. What will we do?'

He continued, gazing at the dark sky where no moon was visible. The city lights were dim, as if lazy or lifeless. It felt like something strange was brewing in the mysterious corridors of fate. My uncle spoke again:

'I can imagine what they'll do. They've started the play, and they won't rest until it's over. Whenever they see something successful, they want to control it and make it theirs alone'

I felt a strong sense of challenge, realizing I needed to lead this crucial battle and win it. I didn't know how, and I lacked the knowledge and tools to take on such a difficult role. But I knew myself—once I set my mind on something, I pursue it relentlessly, convinced of success. I asked my uncle before heading to the mosque for dawn prayer:

'Will you trust me to handle this matter?'

He gave me a loving look. He cared for me deeply—I was sure of it—and trusted me greatly. He had given me opportunities no one else ever had. He said nothing, but his glowing expression assured me I had his trust and the right to act.

My aunt was also anxious. She told us that the politician's wife was cunning and unpredictable. Though a friend, she couldn't be trusted. My aunt repeated:

'Never trust politicians; they have more than one face.'

'I have known her for a long time. She covets anything that shines like gold in others' hands,' she added.

We sat together, my uncle, aunt, and I, trying to figure out a solution, and had delayed going to work that day, the confusion starting early. My uncle looked at my aunt, saying:

'Leave it to our saving hero. Don't worry.'

My aunt smiled—she trusted me. Yet this situation seemed impossible, as her non-welcoming demeanour suggested. She knew that woman better than we did.

Without speaking, we headed to work, while my aunt stayed behind, busying herself with an old hobby—mending clothes—not out of necessity, but to pass the time and ease her anxiety.

At the shop, I focused on my work, but my mind was elsewhere. I had made a promise, and I had to keep it. A solution was needed, and it had to be final, preventing future interference. Once we dealt with this woman and her husband, there would likely be others to contend with.

An idea came to mind, though I wasn't sure it would work. But as the saying goes, 'You never know until you try'.

Around midday, I asked my uncle for permission to start my mission. He didn't ask about my plan, simply granting me permission. He then took over the shop, something he rarely did in my presence, greeting customers and overseeing the finances.

I went home, took a shower, dressed in a sharp blue suit, and applied some cologne. Then I headed straight to the large bank building where my uncle worked. I was telling myself that he might fire me or do something bad. Despite the past incident where I'd ignored him at the party, I told myself I had to try. This is the first step.

Deep down, I believed he would help. I knew he had a good heart, though his wife was another story. These politicians are often ruined by their wives. Maybe this is largely true. I won't bother myself with finding an answer to my question.

Upon arrival, the security guard—that young man who had once scorned me but had since become a friend—recognised me and greeted me warmly. He seemed unaware that I had left my uncle's home, or even if he did, he knew better than to do anything but welcome me. People like him live in fear, blind obedience, and arrogance toward the weak.

I entered my uncle's office. My appearance—sharp suit, shiny shoes—was enough to earn respect. They, too, respect those dressed well. The office manager opened the door for me, and I entered. My uncle was sitting, smoking his pipe as usual, next to a man I thought him was that minister frequently seen on TV and in newspapers, looking thinner in person. Also present was a woman I'd seen the night I was detained, the one clinging to my uncle at that party.

My uncle stood up, warmly greeting me with a hug, as if the incident at the wedding had never happened. I received equally warm welcomes from the minister and the woman, especially after my uncle introduced me:

'This is my nephew—a successful businessman.'

I felt a quiet sense of pride, even if my uncle's words weren't entirely truthful. Apparently, he knew where I had been. Nothing remains hidden in this country. I sat on a sofa, while my uncle moved from his desk to sit beside me. He whispered:

'Your mother was asking about you. She was here a few days ago, but I didn't tell her where you are'

He paused, then added:

'I reassured her that you're not far and that you'll return with plenty of money. He is in a good position.'

I felt a sharp pang in my heart at the mention of my mother, realizing that I wasn't even helping her a little bit. Then I regained my composure and said directly to him:

'I've come to you for a favour, if you're willing to help me.'

He adjusted his seating position, showing interest. He responded:

'At your service... I know you've come for something.'

He took a deep puff of his pipe, his eyes expressing intense interest. He spoke without concern for the others present, and our conversation was audible to them. He added:

'When it comes to a favour and a businessman, there's always a price. In the past, you had nothing, kid.'

He laughed loudly.

I had never seen him act this way before. He seemed to reveal a different side, not the submissive, docile, kind uncle I knew.

The lady also laughed in an inappropriate way, her local tobe slipping down her shoulders, revealing the top of her chest. She was wearing a very short, tight dress. The minister, however, remained expressionless, like a statue.

I admit, I felt uncomfortable and didn't understand the nature of what was happening. Was it mockery? or a praise wrapped in sarcasm?

I stopped thinking when my uncle asked firmly:

'What exactly do you want?'

I told him what had happened, and he listened intently. Then he turned to the minister and asked:

'Did you hear about this story?'

The minister, without looking our way, wiped his dark sunglasses with the edge of his untucked shirt and said:

'This woman is trying to take over land that isn't hers. She's pushing this man into hell.'

My uncle glanced at the woman seated among them, and she seemed to understand his silent message. She responded curtly:

'I'll discipline her. Is that what's needed?'

'Just tell her to stop playing with the big players,' my uncle replied.

The woman took the instruction, and my uncle looked at me saying:

'Any other favours, young capitalist?'

I felt a rush of happiness that my mission had succeeded. I thanked him and, as I was leaving, he walked me to the office door himself, opening it as he said:

'Don't forget your mother… take care.'

It was a sting to my conscience, a reminder that I should do something for her, at least send her some money. But that monster would swallow it all. I knew him well. I let the thought slide as I usually do with things I'd rather forget.

When I reached the shop, my uncle was exhausted and sweating, as it had been a long time since he had managed the work himself. He rushed to embrace me, understanding from my expression as I got out of the taxi in a hurry that I had found a solution. I told him:

'The problem is solved.'

'You went to your uncle, no doubt,' he responded.

There wasn't much to think about—only whether I would have the courage to go to him or not. I did it.

That evening, my aunt was overjoyed at the news. Not long after, the politician's wife arrived to inform us that she had backed off from the matter. Naturally, she didn't tell my aunt the whole story, but my uncle didn't seem entirely comfortable either. After his daytime joy, he was worried again by nightfall. I noticed this and asked him. He told me:

'These people don't do favours for free. We need to figure out what the price is.'

He paused, then added:

'If your uncle stood up for you—or for us—he wouldn't defeat his political friends unless he had a reason.'

I explained a point that I might not have made clear before because I hadn't shared all the details:

'It's about settling scores between them.'

'I know that, son. I've lived long enough to understand. What I mean is, your uncle must be thinking about something.'

I thought hard but couldn't come up with a specific idea. My uncle reassured me:

'Don't worry about it as long as the problem is solved. Let's live normally until something changes.'

He suggested we sleep early since we would go to an important place at dawn before work. I couldn't figure out where until the next day when we took a taxi and headed to the large central prison under the bridge where the Italian worker had buried, completed years ago.

The prison's gate was large, flanked by two concrete boxes on either side where two soldiers with rifles aimed at an unknown target.

It was my first time entering this prison. The last time I was in prison, it wasn't here. This one was reserved for politicians, big businessmen, people with bounced checks, those serving long sentences or life, and those awaiting execution.

We entered a dirty, rundown reception hall. After a while, the fat man arrived, now frail and weak, showing the toll of the past years of suffering. His beard had grown long, though he hadn't had one before. He wore the white prison uniform and embraced us tightly, soaking our clothes with tears each time we tried to pull away.

He said he regretted many things in life, had repented to God, and memorized the Quran in prison, as there was nothing else to occupy him. He had even become the imam for the prisoners, including political leaders who were occasionally brought in.

Looking down at the ground, he told us:

'Time passes quickly, and a person realizes they wasted it on worthless things.'

He patted my shoulder and head, advising me:

'You're in good hands. Obey your uncle and aunt, be grateful to God for your blessings, and don't forget to visit your parents in the town. No matter what, honouring them is your duty.'

Our time with him ended quickly, and as we left, my uncle seemed deeply affected. I couldn't quite define my emotions. Perhaps I felt sad, but this is the nature of life. I told myself this while trying not to succumb to the negative emotions I usually have in these situations. Sometimes I recalled what that psychoanalyst had once said about me, describing me as suffering from an incurable mental illness. Maybe he was right, since I never sought medical help for it.

If the fat man had touched my senses, I knew that soon enough, I would forget even what he had said about my parents. It might have had an impact at first, but it wouldn't linger in my mind for long. My uncle knew this about me and understood my nature, though I'm unsure if he saw it as a strength or a weakness.

On our way back to the shop, I asked him:

'What made you think of visiting him?'

He responded while shielding his face from the thick dust hanging in the air, stirred up by the wind, which was common in this dusty month and the one following, when everything is washed with heavenly dust:

'I've been thinking about it for a long time, but it just got delayed. I'm not sure what made today the right day. What matters is that it happened.'

We didn't discuss the fat man or the prison after that, and life went on as usual, with work taking up most of our time.

Occasionally, I thought about visiting my family in the town for a day, but I either neglected the idea or forgot about it. It's hard to tell. Perhaps my personality was taking shape in a way that I was moulding, or perhaps not. There was no escape from following the path fate had laid out for me. The same was true for sending money to my mother. It never happened. Not because I valued money too much, or because I was struggling financially, or because I was stingy—none of that. It was just that something inside me kept saying it should wait for the right time. Many more years passed before that suitable time came.

6
My uncle's hard times

Perhaps my uncle's instinct was correct in choosing the timing for the visit of the fat man, who no longer remained so. Within less than two months of that visit, developments occurred in the country that accelerated many things that one would never have imagined.

These developments shattered many dreams, lives, and businesses. The president of the country had travelled to the United States for treatment of a mysterious illness that the authorities had not disclosed. This was the same president before whom I once stood in a church holding a wreath of flowers, who seemed as strong as an iron horse, and whom one could hardly imagine becoming frail.

They said his condition had deteriorated beyond hope and no way to save him. The large radio in the shop was not providing any new information and did not address the president's health or the real news that people were whispering in the streets. Instead, it played celebratory messages for obscure occasions and speeches written years ago. Everyone knew that a deception was at play, and the streets were boiling over in a strange way.

Within two days, the big city turned into a collective outcry. Transportation networks and landlines were down, and doctors, drivers, bakers, and pharmacists went on strike. The sick and pregnant women were dying with no one to care for them. This, to me, was a sin.

Within days, everything ended when a frail officer from the army appeared on television and local radio to announce the takeover of power in the country. Such things happen almost regularly in our country since independence and the departure of the British.

We heard about the mass prison break and that everyone had escaped on the night of the coup. It might have been orchestrated by the new authorities, or perhaps it was the freedom that the prisoners had been waiting for, and they found the right moment to seize it, with all gratitude to fate.

Early in the morning, the fat man knocked on our door, and my uncle welcomed him warmly. He had come to bid us a final farewell, as he said. He didn't disclose where he was heading next, only that he didn't trust the future and needed to leave quickly, and he had come just to say goodbye.

We embraced him tightly, and he went on his way. My aunt was also sad and wished he could have stayed to work in the shop, but my uncle explained to her:

'It's too risky. He still has many years left on his sentence. They might arrest him again if he stays here.'

I had imagined on the day he was sentenced that he would leave when he would be nearly eighty years old, and I would be close to forty. But these strange moments came and changed the course of events and reversed many things.

Many men of the old regime and politicians lost their positions, and my uncle was the first among them. We listened to the new appointments on the radio, and my uncle's name was no longer mentioned. I don't know how he feels now. Would he be satisfied? Certainly not! Perhaps he can endure it; I know his nature. But the biggest disaster will befall his wife. How will she cope now that the great man has lost his social status and financial position? I jokingly told my uncle:

'There he goes without getting paid.'

My uncle looked at me in a way that suggested he didn't approve of my comment on the situation. He said:

'We must learn not to mock others. Calamities in this world are shared and circulated among people.'

I felt fear, and I remembered that in the recent past, I had not been happy enough—in fact, I hadn't been happy at all. I need to focus on my own affairs and not waste time thinking about what others have done or will do. These are the tricks of the weak and the failures, as my Turkish uncle warned me.

In the few years following the coup against the president, the country lived through a period of anticipation, and we were all part of it. No matter how much a person thinks he is isolated from the general framework, politics, and government, it affects him. We noticed this directly in our business, which began to experience fluctuations after the prosperity we had enjoyed in recent years.

Customers dwindled for reasons that seemed unclear at first, but we later discovered that most of those who used to come to us had fled the country with their families. Some had escaped the trials announced by the new authorities against everyone identified as symbols of the previous era. Some trials were conducted in absentia, with mass death sentences handed down but not executed because the accused were not present—they couldn't be found.

Others had emigrated because they had lost their positions and preferred to gather what remained of their money in foreign banks and headed for Australia and America in search of safe havens for themselves and their children.

One customer would come to bid us farewell, and then another, and my uncle faced the calamities with patience. The new regime was a disaster, a true divine retribution from which we were among the victims. I remembered my Turkish uncle's advice about my maternal uncle's situation, and here we are, included in the calamity ourselves.

The damage also reached my old friends on the street. Within days, they were rounded up from their various locations, but where they were taken, no one knew.

The new situation seemed more dreadful, but as they say, every cloud has a silver lining. This is what changed the direction of the wind once again, because after several months, the market began to recover again. The new environment nurtured new politicians and other merchants who wore shinier European shoes and spoke English with an American accent.

There was talk about the return of some sons of politicians in exchange for deals with the new regime. Instead of the old politician returning to the country, he would send his son to participate in the government, thus ensuring a 'decent living' for the same groups. Among them was my uncle, as I learned from customers that after he emigrated to Egypt on his way to Western countries, his daughter returned to take up a senior position in one of the ministries, paving the way for the family's return. So the great lady's sadness wouldn't last long.

Perhaps the situation wouldn't be exactly as it was before. I kept telling myself that, and I didn't share such fleeting thoughts with my uncle because he couldn't tolerate this kind of thinking about others' affairs, which he found pointless.

Our patience ended when the situation began to improve again, allowing us to recover the losses we had suffered. If that recovery had been delayed, we might have ended up in prison due to the debts that began to pile up, which the suppliers of livestock, vegetables, and spices were demanding payment for.

My uncle had stopped travelling during that period because the financial situation didn't allow it. Moreover, my aunt, who had begun to hate the country she claimed to have loved more than her homeland, had regained her vitality. She resumed her frequent visits to the beauty salon and was preparing to attend some weddings without me, as work left me no time.

A few weeks later, money began to flow in more than it had before the uprising. The new customers were young people who loved what we offered and enjoyed it. Their tastes were based on new habits, unlike the traditional meals their parents and grandparents were accustomed to in local restaurants. The collective behaviour of eating sandwiches, especially shawarma, became a phenomenon that added to the transformations that occurred in the new era, which reflected well on us.

As a result, my uncle left me for a few days and travelled to see his daughter, as he had been delayed due to the crisis that had almost destroyed our business, leaving me to manage the shop alone.

The addition that took place was that I hired two young Ethiopian workers after much effort. I began training one of them on how to cut and prepare the meat in an organized manner, adding the necessary spices and marinades.

Of course, learning that produces excellent results takes time, as with all matters of life. Therefore, intervention and careful supervision form me were necessary to ensure that the worker understood all the steps and executed them precisely and with great passion.

The second worker's job was to continuously clean the tables and the shop and serve the customers, while I took over the accounting myself, even when my uncle was around, allowing him to relax in his chair, observe the situation, and welcome his beloved customers. Especially since old age had started to affect him—just a year or so ago, he could stand for long hours, but now that was difficult for him. He was also once able to perform hard labour in the back room where preparations were made before arranging the ready meat on the outdoor shawarma machine.

During my uncle's absence, I felt that something was missing, even though being busy with work makes one forget everything, even their sense of self. Once, my uncle described work to me as a true prayer, saying that when one devotes oneself to it sincerely, they are rewarded. He also told me that livelihood flows from true dedication to what a person does.

That was true to a great extent in its personal reflection on me. Whenever I finished long hours of work at night, I would take a deep breath and say, 'Thank God.' At that moment, I would feel a deep joy filling my pores, as if I were flying while awake. I told my uncle about this, and he pointed out that it was a sign of success, as perseverance and hard work ultimately bear fruit that only those who experience toil and effort can taste.

The two workers were learning from me and my uncle. They showed us affection, and I saw in them a level of dedication greater than what I often saw in our own people. Selecting them wasn't easy, which gave me the experience to understand that an employer must spend a long time waiting for a diligent, obedient, and creative worker, and once found, satisfaction is guaranteed. This was my experience.

My uncle entrusted me with the task and didn't interfere. I can say that the selection process took a lot of time and exhausting tests. The principle I relied on, inherited from my uncle, was that 'a good craftsman works with his heart, not just his hands… and so he performs his work with his heart, not just his hands'. Therefore, I had to delve into their hearts to determine who was fit to start working with us.

During that period, I discovered that my peers were looking for work but were unwilling to accept anything less than ideal. They didn't believe that one could start small and expand over time. They wanted the sky to pour all its water at once, wanted emotions to govern instead of reason, all of which go against the laws of life.

They had acquired these attitudes from the chaos in the country, where they saw people rising to high ranks overnight, regardless of qualifications or abilities. Many also lacked something important: a strong will and determination, without which one stands no chance.

As I learned from my uncle, opportunities are created by people themselves; life doesn't operate on coincidences but on hard work and perseverance. There was one final point where most of those who were tested for work with us failed: the ability to sacrifice and forget everything except work. They had to work for the sake of work, not to live another life.

Before my uncle's return—his absence had been prolonged this time—and one night, as I was preparing to leave the shop to head home (my aunt wouldn't sleep until I arrived, as we often chatted together for a while), I noticed a face in the distance. It was unclear at first because I had taken off my glasses while washing my face before I dry it with a tissue. As my vision returned with my glasses on, the figure became more distinct.

It was that young man of vile character, the son of the old guard at my maternal uncle's house. He was still shaven-headed, perhaps he kept it that way always, and he seemed shorter—perhaps he used to wear high shoes.

He stood in front of me cautiously, politely asking to greet me. I extended my hand and shook his, waiting for him to reveal his purpose, for he had surely come for a reason. He didn't seem, in any case, to be the same person who had once been a reason for my abandoning my uncle's house.

I gestured for him to sit, and one of the Ethiopian workers brought him a glass of cold water, which he drank, belching automatically. It didn't seem deliberate. He said to me:

'I hope you'll forgive me for coming here… I know I was…'

I interrupted him, as he was mumbling, not knowing exactly what he wanted to say. He seemed afraid that I would turn him away.

'I understand the situation… What is it that you want now?'

He replied with his head down:

'I'm looking for work… I have no means of income for myself or my family, especially since my father returned to the village after your uncle left…'

'But the daughter has returned, hasn't she? Why don't you work with her?'

'Sorry, sir… We can only work with the great lady'

I recalled his actions that night when he jumped out of the window. In that moment, I saw him naked before me and despised him.

I almost exploded and confronted him with his ugly truth, which he knew all too well, but I chose to be patient and avoid other topics. He had come for a specific purpose, and I had to tell him either yes or no. Life here had taught me this: to be concise and focused on the matter at hand. My uncle had advised me of this in my early days because, sometimes, I would ramble or ask meaningless questions.

The guard's son was waiting for my answer, without having answered my question about why he didn't work with the younger lady. I left him to his own devices, whether to forget the question or ignore it, as he was clearly agitated.

It was a charade to achieve his goal. I knew this type of person well, and I found myself standing from my seat, without hesitation, pointing at him with my finger, sternly and firmly, in a way he didn't expect:

'There's no work for you here... Thank you for your trust.'

To be honest, I couldn't hire him even if he had extraordinary abilities; the shop didn't need more workers. Moreover, my rule was known: competency, which had led me to reject some young men who had been recommended by prominent clients. I didn't care about that and assured my uncle, who knew I wouldn't consider things with any kind of empty sentimentality.

I didn't feel the need to explain or justify myself to the guard's son. I wasn't obligated. He lifted his head with difficulty, muttering something incomprehensible before heading towards the shop's outer door.

Once again, confused images of that disgraceful night flashed before me, intertwined with the moment he twisted my arm, threw me to the ground, stole my money, and kicked me out of the room.

I stared at him intently, probably he understood from my gaze that true victory comes to those who earn it through their own hard work, and that true intelligence lies in the mind, not in rudeness. I felt no sympathy for him. He was dressed in rags like someone who had just climbed out of a sewer. Although I didn't smell any stench from him, my imagination was quick to conjure smells that didn't exist, depending on situations, objects, and people.

That night didn't end well, as the saying goes. This thug wouldn't let things pass like that. His reaction, once he reached the shop's outer door, was to slam his fist violently against the glass, producing a loud noise and shattering part of it. Blood dripped from his fingers as he glared at me savagely, screaming loudly in pain, indicating deep-seated anger before shouting violently:

'Do you think you're something special, you cripple?'

He was mocking my limp, which I had nearly forgotten about. I might have felt a slight twinge in an unknown part of my body, but I ignored it, raising my finger sharply to threaten him:

'Get out of here and wait until your respectable lady returns to work with her.'

He couldn't control himself. He understood that I was implying something specific and charged at me, pushing me backward with both hands. I staggered before regaining my balance with difficulty, narrowly avoiding falling to the ground.

Fortunately, the two Ethiopian workers were watching the situation and, as I had expected, they intervened just in time. They wouldn't allow me to be struck. I was surprised that, despite their frail bodies, they managed to grab him, lift him high, and slam him to the ground.

They would have repeated it had I not signalled them to stop. He had staggered heavily, like a drunk, groping his way along the street, disappearing from sight.

I thought the matter was over, but two nights later, at almost the same time, he returned, more ferocious this time, with a wicked plan that he seemed intent on executing.

Evil doesn't need an introduction, my boy. He arrived at the moment when I was about to close the shop's outer door and leave. The workers had already left. I suspect he had been watching the shop until he was sure of the right time to attack. People like him can only be evil; they were created for that purpose.

As he approached me, and I could barely see clearly due to the dark fog after turning off the external lights, leaving only a small violet-coloured lamp lit until morning, he attacked me swiftly and unexpectedly. He didn't give me time to think about the next moment. He struck my thin body with a sharp dagger, and all I remember is repeatedly screaming, 'Ah.'

I woke up in the hospital days later. I don't know how many days had passed. I was in the same place I had entered the day of that cursed accident in which the limping man died.

Once again, it felt like I was in a dream. I remember I was walking through long tunnels under the river until I entered a distant city where there were dwarves did nothing but jump over trees like monkeys and sing in melodious voices.

There was music playing that I had to follow to see where it would lead me. My father who became old was driving his battered government car, while a truck carrying our family from the village, neighbours, and many relatives threw them all into a deep pit and buried them with soil.

It was hard to understand the connection between the music and the dwarves with those last images. The important thing was that they were dreams, and logic often didn't apply to them.

I saw my uncle standing beside me, gently touching my curly hair, which had grown long, saying:

'Thank God you're safe… You almost died if it weren't for God's mercy.'

My aunt was shedding tears of joy, and I was in a state of mental absence, unable to speak, struggling to articulate words.

My uncle signalled me to rest, assuring me that everything would be fine in its own time. A nurse came in with a long needle and injected me in my buttock, and I slipped into a coma once again.

Weeks passed in the hospital, and during that time, old images of the town, my siblings, my father, and my mother reappeared in my dreams. This time, I was chasing their ghosts in very long and high walls as if they were movie screens. I discovered that I was standing in a desert with no one around but myself. I woke up to find my uncle and aunt by my side. I told them:

'I'm scared and disturbed... I'm haunted by troubling nightmares.'

'You will be fine... This is normal after what happened to you,' my uncle said.

'And where is that...?'

'He fled. No one saw him, and the police haven't found him'

One afternoon, after I had recovered, I stayed at home for days, doing nothing but reading those books I love about personal development and success in life.

Walking was difficult in the first days due to a curvature in my back and sharp pains, to the extent that I had to urinate in the room.

I didn't know what that wretched man had done to make his dagger wound my back after turning my belly into a strange map. I feared continuing in this condition, adding another disability to myself.

The nightmares had stopped after I felt that life must go on and that I would not be stuck at this step. I would not go back. I had read in one of the books with me that people sometimes romanticize their past, but often this is a false emotion that one needs to overcome. The truth lies in the present moments and the future. No one can support us in being strong except ourselves, no matter the degree of kinship or affection.

For an unknown reason I did not fully understand, I continued to feel that I might have committed a major sin deserving of atonement someday, but the right time had not yet come.

It was difficult for me to think clearly by myself. It was not about time, but about a sensitivity I lacked, originating from solitude and pure clarity, that mysterious and exciting thing that makes you see certain things in their true light at a particular moment. This happens under certain circumstances and at times we cannot choose.

I didn't think of discussing this with my uncle. I preferred to be brave and continue being myself, not a borrowed person from the past or memories or overwhelming desires that might take us back to an old point and find ourselves in a difficult situation. The essence of being human is to remain resilient until the end.

During my absence from work, the shop was run by my uncle and the Ethiopian workers, but the pace weakened as I later learned. My uncle and aunt were hiding this because they knew I would go to the shop in any way I could if I knew.

When I returned, my back had a slight curvature. The doctor said it would improve over time with some exercises and physical therapy. Customers had missed me during this period, and in reality, some had visited me in the hospital or at home or at least asked about me. I was active and felt a doubled challenge that I had to be better. If I had been struck by a blow, I would not stand still; I had to keep moving and persevering.

My uncle welcomed me back to the shop saying:

'Everyone has been looking forward to your return… Welcome, my son.'

I glanced at the shop, scrutinized the details, and felt how much I loved this place with everything in it. I knew it completely. It was my miniature and grand world. My uncle was observing me and feeling what I felt, and he began to rejoice.

My aunt was also present, witnessing this day as a celebration. On the first day, I worked less, which was normal. Days passed, and my activity increased, finding my mind crowded with ideas I needed to implement from those I had accumulated during the recovery period, mixed with what I read in books and some wandering dreams. All of this mixed in my head in the form of plans and tasks that needed to be done immediately, at least the important ones.

A week passed, then two weeks, a month, and two months. The shop thrived, but my uncle reduced his presence due to feeling tired. I did not know how fate worked in this world, but as soon as I returned to the shop, the fatigue syndrome began to haunt my uncle.

He was brave in resisting the pain, but illnesses do not respect spirits or the courage of their bearers. They continue to invade until they declare victory. That was some of my uncle's wisdom as he lay in bed at home, suffering from recurring joint and bone pains, perhaps due to years of hard work, the journey of life he had lived until this moment.

He asked me one night as I was returning from the shop:

'What about your new ideas? We haven't seen anything yet!'

I took a quick and careful glance at his exposed face between his fully covered body with a woollen blanket, even though the weather was not very cold. In reality, he was not asking me; he was trying to show a kind of resistance to the pain and the feeling that this body had a limited lifespan before it should rest in eternal sleep.

I don't know why these troubling thoughts haunted me as I looked at his face, which had become wrinkled and saggy, while his small, difficult smile revealed deep sadness, perhaps a feeling that life, as beautiful and full of adventures and joys as it is, falters in some areas and becomes painful and harsh, making escape from it preferable. We do not often make that decision; it is always life that decides for us and prevails with its eternal will.

My uncle repeated his question with difficulty this time, and I understood more deeply that he was searching for something to hold on to hope in this world, that someone would carry his torch.

I dressed in his wisdom and applied it to my thoughts and how I perceived and evaluated the events around me. I answered him:

'I will do everything to make you happy, uncle... very soon.'

I found myself saying without a pre-planned strategy:

'We will open another new shop soon.'

This statement had no basis other than that it came out at that moment and became a challenge I had to succeed in achieving to make my uncle happy.

Indeed, three months passed, and my uncle was at home fighting increasing pains. Sometimes we would take him to the doctor for routine procedures and return. Sometimes doctors only play a formal role, offering apologies for the bad weather or the poor quality of medicines in the country, due to the blockade imposed by advanced countries on our nation, claiming that the new rulers are part of the international terrorism network, even if they have studied and grown up in their own country.

During these three months, the dream came true. The new shop was ready. I began by choosing a location near the confluence of the two rivers at the base of the new bridge. They had built more bridges to accommodate the increasing number of displaced people using public transportation to reach the city center, where everyone is searching for a livelihood. In that area, there were hotels frequented by foreigners and many cafes where competition might be tough, but I believed that success comes amidst difficulties and not in easy places.

The shop's rent was high, but my calculation was that we would succeed in achieving higher returns in an area described as touristy.

I equipped the shop with modern décor, bright colours, and colourful lights, and the large picture of either me or my late cousin, the Turkish, was redrawn here, becoming a distinctive mark and logo for us, just like the famous American Kentucky Fried Chicken. The difference here was the portrait of a young man with curly hair, while there it was an older man.

Throughout this period, I left the Ethiopian workers to run the old shop, and they performed well while I was almost entirely dedicated to the new shop's setup.

Everything went according to the plan I had drawn in my mind since that night when I announced it to my uncle. That night, until dawn, I didn't sleep as I had drawn the entire plan, from choosing the shop to its final appearance to my vision of customers moving inside it, including my maternal cousin's daughter. We had held an opening party, which was a great event in the big city, similar to many events for the influential class.

What preoccupied me was reaching the final point before something unfortunate happened, God forbid. There was a mysterious feeling haunting me that my uncle was at the end of his journey. This matter was difficult to get rid of, to the extent that I began to doubt my own nature. Was I an evil and devilish being creating such unpleasant imaginations? Is it true that there are devils whispering to us, separating us from our true emotions and the goodness within us? Or do we have counterparts working against us with all their might and power?

I resisted the evils of my soul and my audacity to the extent that I sometimes imagined my uncle had died, and I inherited everything. I would drift into fantasies that did not please me and try to chase them away, but they would return to me frequently and sometimes intensely.

My aunt was aware of my plans and the ongoing preparations. She didn't have enough time to notice the daily progress because she was busy taking care of my uncle. However, she at least asked about and checked on the surprise I was preparing for him.

Once, she even came with me to see how the shop was nearly ready. We set the date for this important event in the same way I had planned it that night when I completed the plan.

The day of the opening arrived. My uncle came to witness the happy occasion. Despite his pain and discomfort, he was joyful, as if he were returning to life, strong and youthful. The area in front of the new shop was filled with guests, including regular customers, some important entities, and community figures. Virtually no one was late. The night went wonderfully as I had imagined, with one difference: my maternal cousin wasn't there as I had envisioned.

Late at night, after everything was done, my uncle said to me at home:

'You have done something wonderful, my son. I am overwhelmed with happiness. You are a true pride to me. I want to tell you a secret I have kept from you for a long time, and now is the right moment to reveal it.'

I was expecting something specific, related to the old news about the will. Indeed, he told me:

'I have allocated a certificate in your name at the court, in appreciation of your efforts and dedication over the years you have worked with me. But in reality, you are more than that. You are a true son.'

I saw him crying as he had never done before. His tears flowed onto the blanket. He was coughing heavily, and I was worried for him, not knowing how to respond. What could I say? My ability to speak seemed to falter. It was a feeling that is hard to describe, even after many years.

Sometimes, one finds that their life is shaped in a place other than what they expect. This happened to me.

For a moment, as I embraced my uncle, I wondered who I was. What was my real relationship to this moment in time? Was it present and real, or was it just a figment of imagination? Had I grown up, or was I still that little boy who feared seeing his mother being hit at night, resisting the idea of waking up to escape into dreams to escape the bitterness of reality? Maybe I was still within one of those dreams, and my existence was just a dream. Even this night and the opening of the new shop.

It was not a dream; it was life as it should be. Regardless of the results, the past cannot be erased, and the lesson is to move forward into the future. It was as if a voice inside me was telling me that this was my reality that I must hold onto.

The next morning, despite having slept only a few hours, I was active, strong, and alert. I had to hurry through a long list of tasks that needed to be done after the shop's opening, as duties had multiplied.

On my way, the airport square was crowded with people. It seemed there was a major event taking place. In reality, I don't follow external events much, as I am busy with work and family. I focus on what affects us and what I hear from customers to avoid any negative impact on our affairs.

There was noise and loud voices shouting, 'Long live… long live…' I understood that they were chanting for the former president, who had gone to America for treatment. I knew he would return to the country at noon, and people had flocked to welcome him, after having demanded his ouster, a while ago asking to execute him in a large demonstration after his regime collapsed.

The taxi driver talked to me about how people in this country cling to illusions. They don't know or understand what will happen tomorrow. They hate something and get rid of it, only to welcome it back again. In any case, nothing new happens.

The city streets were almost empty. Even the street boys had rushed to the airport to see the miraculous man, as the morning newspapers had called him.

I was absorbed in my thoughts about my uncle's health and the future of the business, wondering how the coming conditions would be. The only thing that concerned me was whether the return of the former president and the overwhelming enthusiasm with which he was received would affect my work. That was all that mattered to me. Everything else was of no significance.

My thoughts were interrupted by the taxi driver's ongoing speculations:

'They say he will take the position of Prime Minister; a new role being invented to create political balance.'

'There's another story that he will run in the next election. Do you think he will win it? Will these crowds actually vote for him, or will they forget in two days? Life is starting to pressure this country, my son, and people want someone to feed them. Do you hear me?' he added.

I was lost in my own matters, and the taxi stopped. I hurried to the new shop. On this day, the customers were fewer; only some who were dissatisfied with the morning's events came by, how people suddenly kicked the whole past and moved to restore it again. One of them was saying:

'Will this old man come back to rule us again? I don't think he is able to speak.'

The day passed very slowly, and I had to end it to go home and see my uncle before heading to the other shop. This had become my daily routine as my uncle's health continued to worry me. Although I hoped the new shop would have a positive impact on him, there was no significant improvement in the immediate aspects.

While he seemed happy and stable, it was not enough to provide a good indication of what the future held. I thought about suggesting that my uncle go to Turkey, where medical care might be better, especially since good doctors had left the country for abroad. Salaries were no longer sufficient, and the situation was deteriorating. I was afraid to bring up this idea with him, knowing how much he loved this place. So, I decided to discuss it with my aunt first. I said to her:

'Are we going to leave Dad in this state here? The situation here isn't good.'

'I think so. What can we do? What do you suggest?' she replied sadly.

'Travelling abroad.'

'I thought of that, but the problem isn't just about temporary treatment. He needs continuous care, which means a long time, and we don't know how long it will last...'

She paused for a moment and then added:

'In any case, he won't be more comfortable anywhere in the world than here. I know that well.'

I realised that what my uncle was suffering from was not a specific illness that could be treated within a set time frame, but rather the accumulation of years of life that suddenly led to all these pains. He was patient, no doubt, but proper care has a role in alleviating pain and helping one live better.

This was on my mind, and my aunt seemed to share the same thoughts. Our visions aligned. We agreed initially, but where would we go, and what would the next plan be? How long would it last, and how would we handle things here? I suggested what I had in mind from the beginning:

'Could Turkey be the right place?'

My aunt looked at me, and I couldn't predict her reaction. Her look was one of surprise and unfamiliarity. She asked:

'What exactly do you mean?'

'I mean, being close to his daughter.'

She shook her head vigorously, as if she were dizzy, and said:

'That cannot happen. He would not be better there.'

Could I ask her about the reason? I hesitated since she had not explained the rest of the matter. Why wouldn't he be happy if he went to his country and was with his daughter? I knew he loved her very much. He used to travel to see her occasionally, and in his last visit, he spent a considerable amount of time with her. So, what was the insurmountable issue preventing that?

My aunt had read the visible confusion on my face and silenced my questions, saying:

'There are things you may not know, my son. They are related to an old history that doesn't necessarily need to be said now, as it's not important for you.'

That increased my confusion. I understood there was something unknown to me about the history of this family. They considered me a son and had given me affection, kindness, and almost everything. Also, at least half of their wealth. However, much of the distant past, and perhaps the recent past, was not clear to me. My uncle's history, his relationship with his country, which I began to understand for the first time from my aunt's scattered hints, indicated that he didn't like it much or preferred to be here. He went there reluctantly for his daughter and to arrange other family matters. It seemed like a debt or atonement for something that happened a long time ago.

I heard from my aunt every day a new addition explaining another aspect or reason why my uncle could not travel to stay with his daughter in Turkey. There was a clear hint not to tell him anything about this matter, so as not to complicate his health situation.

Often, we think we understand certain things because we are part of them or because they shape our lives, but the truth is often the exact opposite. Over time, we have to discover that there are things that are missing and unknown to us. This is life most of the time, in any situation.

My uncle used to repeat a saying like this, that applies to me today. Did he mean something specific? I'm not sure. It was his way of expressing certain judgments, commenting that they might not necessarily be true in all cases. There is what is right in a certain situation and specific circumstances, and that same thing might be wrong in other circumstances.

My aunt and I decided to remain silent about my uncle's condition, letting fate weave its course.

Despite being absorbed in the minutiae of routine life, where time sometimes seems to stand still due to distress, I reserved part of my time, especially at night, for my uncle who despite his illness and his rarely leaving the bed, would stay up late and sleep during the day.

He found solace in reading, placing his daughter's works beside him, which made me feel that he was seeing through them worlds I couldn't access or understand, perhaps some of his lost longings or a yearning for the unknown, the mysterious.

Sometimes he would open a particular page and ask me to read to him. I would start reading in Turkish, stopping over some words in pronunciation but understanding the meaning clearly and transparently, without stumbling.

Although I hadn't read all these books or completed them fully, I knew their general context from my uncle's discussions. They revolve around a rapidly changing country, its tug-of-war between East and West, and new generations trying to kick away the past and embrace the future with dreams different from those inherited.

However, what struck me most was the novel my uncle favoured and asked me to read to him. It tells the story of a father who moves from rural Turkey to the big city in search of a better life and encounters many stories and tales that make him dislike his homeland until he emigrates to another country to find himself and his new life, but the new country is unnamed as if it were speaking about my uncle's life experience.

Once, after reading a passage from the end of a chapter discussing how life among strangers can sometimes make a person happy, I asked him:

'Do you see yourself in this story?'

He gave me a look with a slight smile. Illness had prevented him from revealing his beautiful face, which had once been expressive and strong. He said in a broken, hoarse voice:

'Perhaps... perhaps that's true.'

He didn't elaborate further, while I believed he had much more to say. I raised my voice and read the beginning of the first chapter of the book:

'...I lived a story similar to yours, which is why I understand your situation well. In my childhood, I fled from my family in Antalya, in the southwest of my country, and arrived in Istanbul after a gruelling journey, to start making a life for myself... but in another country.'

Here was someone talking to tell his story to another unknown person, and the narrator said he lived a story similar to that of the listener, but he didn't tell it to him.

I thought about how human experiences are so similar and how this story might resemble my own situation. Such thoughts exhausted me, and I tried to avoid them to prevent falling into the deep wound occupying a part of my soul.

Perhaps my uncle felt the same emotions. I often saw myself as a miniature version of him, as if I were truly his child. It was a strange kind of relationship that can only be understood by those who live it. It's hard for people to believe what they haven't experienced, my dear.

After several months, the daughter arrived. It was necessary to inform her of what was happening and the severity of her father's condition, especially in the recent period, as movement had become difficult for him, and he was almost bedridden for most of the day. The doctors did nothing significant. One of them would come almost daily, set up his equipment, perform his routine work—blood pressure measurements, injections, repetitive advice—and the situation remained the same.

One day, before the daughter and her husband arrived, the doctor said to me:

'I want to tell you something about your father...'

He seemed hesitant, and I asked him to summarize his feelings and tell me what he wanted to express. He said:

'Your father has an incurable disease... recovery is difficult...'

'Do you mean...'

'Yes, my dear. Unfortunately, it's God's will and destiny. What can one do against divine will? I will do what I can...'

For a few minutes, I felt a shiver in my body. I was scared as I had never been before, meaning the inevitable end was approaching. My aunt also felt it, and I didn't know if the doctor had informed her or not. I certainly couldn't tell her.

My uncle was happy to see his daughter, who resembled me to some extent, as in her picture hanging in the house. The sadness in her expression in the picture was absent in reality. She loved life, was graceful, and had a light spirit.

Despite her father's difficult condition, she smiled, and I don't think it was a forced smile. This didn't mean she was unemotional. Sometimes I saw her crying as she lay beside him, hugging him. She tried to hide such feelings from my aunt and me.

Her husband, whom I initially judged unworthy of her, seemed round-faced, short, and somewhat overweight. I learned he worked as a jeweller and wore a large gold earring in his left ear, hanging at least five centimeters. He didn't stay long at the house, leaving in the morning and not returning until late at night, never telling anyone where he went in a country he knew nothing about.

She didn't spend time with him. Was this how their life always was in their country? I couldn't speculate. Although I wasn't comfortable with him, he was kind to me, joking with me in Turkish and promising to make a set of fine jewellery as a gift for my future spouse when I decide to marry.

The jeweller, with his earring, seemed to enjoy life as if he were on a recreational trip, indifferent to the family matters and my uncle's worsening condition.

We all lived in great pain seeing that once bright face now yellowed and its owner unable to speak even a word.

For the daughter, over the week, her condition changed, and she lost some weight, which was noticeable.

My aunt would lock herself in the room, crying alone while hugging a picture of my uncle, describing him with the most beautiful traits as women in my country do when a man dies, whether husband, brother, or close relative.

The situation worsened, affecting my work, which didn't stop but was affected by my frequent absences as I stayed to monitor the intractable condition, as the doctor had said. Every time the doctor came and went, he would glance at me as if saying that only a few hours remained.

The jeweller continued his trivialities, only returning late at night and often being drunk. He would enter the large living room, lie on the sofa, smoke cigarettes voraciously, and sleep until dawn in that spot, his head resting on his knees. He would wake up occasionally, as if dreaming, asking himself:

'Is the uncle okay? Is he okay?'

He would repeat this and then continue sleeping, only to wake up again to speak to an unknown being and end this state by cursing my uncle:

'Let this old man go to hell... He's wasting our time.'

This behaviour was strange to me. It was an odd conduct unbecoming of a respectable person. That's how I classified what I saw.

The daughter seemed indifferent or didn't care about it. Once, I thought of asking her about her relationship with this eccentric man but dropped the idea as the circumstances weren't suitable now.

In the morning, the man went about his usual routine but never entered my uncle's room or looked in his direction. He asked for tea, coffee, juices, and food, only concerned with eating and drinking. No one cared for him. He would shout a lot and eventually enter the kitchen himself, bringing a large tray with what he desired. He would come out in his short underwear, showing off his muscular body decorated with shapes, squares, triangles, and animals like snakes. He would finish the food on the tray, wipe his hands, and leave the utensils where they were.

He would enter the bathroom, and the sound of his flatulence and farts could be heard in the outer hall. He engaged in this barbaric behaviour, then quickly dressed without tucking in his pants or grooming himself and left, not to be seen again until late at night.

The situation wasn't just about my uncle but also the imbecile man who arrived one early evening with a group of young men who resembled him in size, shape, and earrings. I wondered when he met this carefully selected group, as if they had been cast from the same mould. They stayed up in the outdoor area of the house, singing, laughing loudly, and drinking local wine made from palm dates.

It was strange that they communicated since they supposedly didn't know Turkish, and the jeweller knew only that language, as far as I knew. To my surprise, he called me despite my visible displeasure and said:

'These are old friends who studied with me in Istanbul. I gathered them here today to celebrate old times. I never thought we would meet again'

He paused for a moment, seeming composed despite his obvious drunkenness, and continued:

'Tell that old man thank you for being so ill. Otherwise, we wouldn't have met old friends.'

The young men greeted me with strong hands and appeared cheerful, contrary to their initially intimidating or evil appearance. One of them said to me:

'We know you, but you may not know or remember us. We visited the shop many times.'

It was hard for me to recall every customer who came to us. I knew many, but these faces, despite their distinctive features, were not easy to remember.

I thought to myself that they might be lying, and I didn't comment, as I was very upset by the jeweller's comments about my uncle. I went into the house and told my aunt what I saw, saying:

'This situation is unbearable. He shamelessly curses us.'

She had been observing everything from the beginning, but never commented on the situation. I know my aunt well—if she had wanted to stir up trouble, she would have done so. She clearly didn't want to complicate matters, especially given my uncle's health condition.

'I know how to handle people like this... just leave it for now,' she calmly said to me.

I obeyed her, and went to work. That evening, which felt unusually cold, with dark clouds gathering in the sky hinting at ominous possibilities, I was left pondering. Since childhood, the sky's dome has always seemed like an omen to me—predicting events that often come true.

Strange visions began to mix in my mind: images of the man with the earring stabbing me with a sharp dagger, much like the old guard's son had done. I saw him fiercer than I ever expected. His smiles and jokes toward me had transformed into something terrifying.

I pushed those thoughts aside and stayed longer than usual in the old shop, reviewing some ledgers and accounts, not because I had to, but because a vague anxiety gnawed at me, and I couldn't pinpoint its source—perhaps the thoughts I'd had earlier or some inner turmoil I couldn't grasp. Sometimes, a person cannot identify the real causes of their emotional pain and tension.

My intuition was right. At the time I should have been closing the outer door, the man with the earring appeared in front of me, drunk and swaying. He didn't have the same familiar face I knew. He was scowling, his eyes absorbing the scattered streetlights. He was holding a gun, though I didn't know where he got it from, and he threatened me, saying:

'Why did you go and complain to her? Do you think I don't understand? If she had wanted to intervene, she would have done so from the start, but it was you who stirred up the situation.'

I responded calmly and politely, without showing any irritation:

'I understand, but you can talk to me directly. What's the need for a gun?'

He laughed, tilting his head foolishly, and I thought he might be mentally unstable. He said to me:

'I'm the grandson of one of the most famous jewellers in Turkey... you filthy slave. Do you know Turkey? Have you heard of it, you insolent fool? My grandfather once ruled over your ancestors here. Have you read that in history? But clearly, you don't know, because like that old donkey, you never went to school.'

The situation was complicated. He insulted me and my uncle. I could have told him, 'Do you know about Imam Mahdi who expelled your grandfather and his armies from here in utter defeat? That's the history you're ignorant of.'

I heard him continue:

'One bracelet from my shops is worth more than your pathetic life you bastard.'

In that moment, as he waved the gun around, swaying as if about to pull the trigger—and he might have done so—I leaped as high as I could on my good leg, jumping backwards slightly, and slapped him hard across his right cheek. He fell to the ground, and the gun slid far from him.

I picked up the gun, put it in my pocket, locked up the shop, and walked home without paying him any further attention. When I glanced back once, I saw him getting up sluggishly, dragging his feet.

About half an hour after I returned home, I sat in the outer courtyard in one of the chairs, where his friends had gathered earlier in the evening. I heard the main gate slam, and then his shouting became audible—he was cursing my uncle, my aunt, and me. My cousin was watching him, showing no concern about what was happening. Seeing my annoyance and frustration, she said calmly:

'Leave him; he's always like this. He'll come to his senses soon.'

I didn't tell her that he had come to kill me, nor did I mention it at all. Her reassuring smile was enough to give me a sense of peace, holding back any dark thoughts toward her strange-tempered husband.

She gently took him by the hand, and he followed her without objection. She led him into an inner room they had been using since they arrived and closed the door. A few minutes later, she came back to apologise, saying:

'He's like this... he's been suffering from a psychological crisis for many years. Don't blame him.'

Was she implying that he had a mental illness or some other issue, or was she just trying to gloss over what had happened with this apology?

I accepted her apology, especially since she wasn't to blame for bearing the burden of this unfortunate man.

She sat next to me and lit a cigarette, looking thoughtful as a sudden sadness etched itself into her face. She stared into the dark, empty space ahead, forcefully flicking her cigarette on the ground as if consumed by a desire for revenge only she could understand.

I didn't feel the need to talk to her and let her stay in her state. It seemed that this man troubled her deeply, especially since she was a sensitive person, as evident in her natural inclination toward literature, art, poetry, and kindness—something her father often spoke of and admired in her.

I observed her from a distance amidst this sorrowful atmosphere and saw how her small face bore a distinct resemblance to my uncle's features, which had become more pronounced in recent years.

I imagined her as a true sister. Her temperament seemed similar to mine; perhaps we had both inherited traits from my uncle, even though she hadn't spent as much time with him as I had.

In a fleeting moment, a strange urge came over me to hold her close. All these years, I had been so preoccupied with work, day and night, that I hadn't taken the time to truly see a woman as I should. Why was this happening now, especially with someone who was supposed to be like a sister to me and at least fifteen years older? Yet, certain human emotions are impossible to rid oneself of.

I resisted the strange idea that washed over me—the urge to hug her tightly. I wasn't sure how she would react, and the timing wasn't right.

I fought back with all my strength the pull I felt toward her captivating beauty, her lips tinted a faint red in the dim light, and my desire to kiss her in any way possible.

I quickly stood up, walked to the outer gate, paused for a moment, then strolled down the street beside the house, trying to shake off this demonic urge I had never experienced before. I kept asking myself:

'What is happening to me? Is this some sort of retaliation against her rude husband?'

That didn't seem right; she was a different being altogether. She was real flesh and blood, while he was filth.

Only after exhausting myself from walking did I return to the house, needing to sleep.

I entered the house to find her in the same spot, not having moved. She asked me:

'Where did you go? I needed someone to talk to... Aunt isn't here today.'

'By the way, where is she? Where did she go?'

'I don't know. She didn't tell me. She just said she'd be very late, maybe not even coming back until the next day.'

I knew my aunt wasn't particularly fond of her, but she didn't despise her either. My aunt is the kind of person who either loves someone completely or doesn't think about them at all. Hatred rarely enters her heart. She has a philosophy that someone who hates doesn't truly know how to love or appreciate others.

I excused myself to check on my uncle. I hadn't seen him since around noon. He was asleep in his room, his body covered as if in eternal slumber. He snored softly, like the distant hiss of wind. The air from a small desk fan nearby blew softly over him. He loved having it on all night, even when it was cold.

I gently uncovered his face to see him sweating profusely. I kissed his forehead, and when I looked up, I noticed his daughter standing right behind me, watching everything I was doing. Despite the dim light in the room, I could clearly see the tears streaming down her face. It was probably the deep yearning for her father, who now rarely spoke and whose body had withered away.

We both cried at that moment, unable to control ourselves. I didn't fully understand what was happening, but she rushed to embrace me instead of the other way around. She held me tightly. It wasn't out of lust or momentary amusement; it was a different feeling, a kind of warmth that reminded me of the bond you feel with a true sibling, or the love you have for a parent and family.

I felt strongly that this was my family, that this was my sister. My heart raced, and I wasn't lying to myself about my feelings. She, too, shared that same strange human connection, where the body craves the presence of another for some unknown reason beyond fleeting moments.

She took my hand, squeezing it tightly, and we sat together again in the outer courtyard. She said:

'I don't know how to thank you for loving my father. You're a noble young man.'

I didn't know how to respond. Sometimes praise demands silence because there's nothing more you can say. I heard her continue:

'My father loves you very much. I'm not exaggerating when I say his love for you might even surpass his love for me. Many times, when he visited us in Turkey, he would remember you and praise you, talking about you as if you were a blessing from heaven'

She smiled through her tears, still flowing, and gently patted my cheek:

'What's your secret? You're still so young, with many years ahead of you, but you're smart, energetic, and determined to be yourself.'

I felt she had inherited her father's wisdom. It seemed like a family trait. She wanted to share so much with me. Was she searching for someone to listen, having been mostly silent since arriving here? Or had she truly grown fond of me, opening up with details that weren't necessary to reveal at first?

She told me she had married the man with the earring because she genuinely loved him. He was about five years older than her. He had lived next door to her mother's family in two neighbouring buildings. He would drive her to work at the newspaper office where she worked. That happened after their relationship developed. The story was long. The important thing was that the two families got to know each other, and the relationship deepened. But over time, she realised the depth of the wound she had fallen into when it was too late. He suffered from a severe hereditary neurological disorder, which ran in his family—his mother, father, and siblings all had it.

She kept crying without letting go of my hand as she explained:

'I truly loved him, and it was too hard to back out after all those years. That wasn't an option. I couldn't imagine living without him. His illness, which flared up from time to time, only made me feel even more compassion for him. He's a sensitive, kind, and wonderful person. His close friends know this, and that's why they don't mind his behaviour.'

'Does my aunt know about this?'

'No, she doesn't know anything about us—neither me nor him. That's probably why she's irritated by him.'

'So, I shouldn't be mad at him? Do you know what he did to me?'

'No, but he's capable of anything. What happened? Did he spit at you? Curse you, maybe?'

'No. He threatened to kill me. He came at me with a gun as I was leaving the shop.'

She burst into laughter, more than I had ever seen her laugh before. She explained:

'That gun doesn't have a single bullet in it. He carries it around most of the time, threatening anyone he feels like. Believe me, he couldn't kill a fly. It's just his illness.'

'But what if there was a bullet? Wouldn't he pull the trigger? Wouldn't he kill someone?'

She paused for a moment and then replied:

'It's possible. If that happened, the situation would be very different. The important thing is that you're okay now. Watch what he does tomorrow. Believe me, he loves you very much. He knows your story and how much my father loves you.'

'But he curses my uncle a lot.'

'That's his condition. Even when my father visits us, he does the same. But my father understands completely. He's afraid my father will take me away from him. He knows very well that he's sick, and that might lead to an unfortunate outcome, God forbid, making my father take action against him. Of course, he imagines things that will never happen.'

'But didn't you try treatment? A psychiatric clinic?'

'He's been in treatment for years. His condition has improved a lot compared to the past, but full recovery, as the supervising doctor says, will take more time. The doctor recommends we don't restrict his movements or actions, to let him behave like a child.'

'Is that why you don't ask him where he goes or interfere in his matters?'

'More or less, yes. But I think about him a lot. I really do.'

At that moment, I thought to myself that I would have made a terrible mistake if I had done anything reckless in that moment of temptation. The outcome would have been disastrous for me. Thank God I passed through that situation unharmed. The woman loves her husband deeply, and she loves me too, but in a different way. She sees me as a brother, not as a lustful being. Even though I've been confident in my looks since that day the great lady mentioned how handsome I am, and told me about my handsome face… it's true that I limp and have a slightly hunched back, but I know I can still charm women. I'm aware of that about myself.

I asked her permission to go to sleep, as it was late and I had a lot of work in the morning. She was the one who kissed me on the cheek. I felt the softness of her touch but didn't think beyond that.

I hurried to my room, calm and at peace, thinking about her all night, alternating between wakefulness and dreams. I wished my future wife, whoever she might be, would resemble her somehow, take after her looks, her eyes, and the spirit that had filled me.

Her image stayed with me until I woke up in the morning to find the man with the earring standing in the middle of the living room, yawning. He greeted me as if nothing had happened the night before. I thought to myself, his wife is right—he really does have some psychological condition that she understands well and knows how to manage. God help her.

Before heading to work, I checked on my uncle. His eyes were half-closed. That early morning, something seemed amiss. Something new was happening in the country. People whispered about a military faction taking control of the situation in the capital, and a battalion coming from distant regions to restore order. Soldiers were everywhere, and tanks filled the streets. When had they gathered in such numbers?

When I returned home the night before, after leaving the man with the earring lying on the ground, the streets were quiet, lit only by scattered streetlights. But that's life here—at any moment, the military might seize control under the pretext that corruption has spread and the country is in a dark tunnel.

I couldn't reach our second shop next to the confluence of the two rivers, so I walked home, covering long distances until I was exhausted.

The checkpoints were numerous, spaced only meters apart, with rifles aimed at anyone who failed to comply with the orders of army officers issuing commands from their high, tiger-striped green vehicles.

When I got home, the man with the earring was sitting in front of the small television in the living room. He jumped up and told me excitedly:

'A new general has taken power in your country... Congratulations!'

I almost replied, 'No surprise, that's what we're used to. Ever since independence, we've gone from one general to another.' I asked him:

'What's his name?'

But I knew the name didn't matter. Those who suddenly appear on the screen or stage are often nobodies from the past. No one knows where they come from.

His voice pierced through the noise and chanting from the nearby street, which made it hard to understand exactly what was being said. It seemed like the military blockade on the streets had ended.

'They call him 'the ruthless hawk...' That's how they introduced him on TV.'

'You mean they didn't mention his real name?'

'Maybe they did, but I didn't pay attention. The presenter kept repeating the phrase 'the ruthless hawk.'

That name stirred something in me. It felt like I had heard it before. Sometimes we hear names or see people and feel as if we've encountered them before. Was I certain I had heard this name? Was he one of the distinguished army officers who visited our shop late at night, ordering large amounts of food and then disappearing into the darkness, only to return days later?

I couldn't come to a clear conclusion and dismissed the thought as a mere figment of my imagination. After all, many people could be called 'the ruthless hawk'.

The man with the earring was as jubilant as if the coup had happened in his own country or as if he were a partner in the new government. He dashed outside, picking up a stick from the fallen neem tree branches near the gate, and hurried into the street.

We could hear his voice joining the crowd, chanting, as they marched past the house, clearly visible through the living room windows. They raced by, carrying coloured flags and wearing headbands. My cousin looked at me, shaking her head in a mixture of amazement and joy, saying:

'That's just how he is, and he will never change'

After a brief pause she added:

'Anyway, this is a historic moment for your country. I will write about it one day in one of my books.'

As she moved closer to stand by me at the window, she asked:

'Would you like me to write a book about you, telling your story?'

I glanced back at her and saw how close she was standing, a fragrant, pleasant scent emanating from her. I loved that fragrance, which became etched in my memory as a symbol of this 'historic day' as she called it.

I showed my appreciation for her idea through my facial expressions, even though I didn't know much about books that tell stories.

The day passed without work, as the celebrations lasted until the evening, and the man with the earring returned late, as did my aunt. we did not know where she had gone. She rarely disappeared without a reason. My uncle was alone in his room, his coughing sound rising and then gradually subsiding.

By dawn the next day, the streets had calmed because the new government had imposed a curfew. An hour or so before that, the man with the earring had returned, exhausted, and collapsed into a deep sleep on the couch, cursing the new general non-stop. This time, my uncle was spared from his insults.

Then my aunt appeared, she was exhausted and rushed to her room, and locked it without speaking to us, she just said hello.

My cousin and I didn't quite understand what was going on, so we waited, suspecting that her absence had something to do with my uncle's illness. Perhaps she was looking for a cure from one of those religious healers she believed in or consulting one of the women she trusted in spiritual matters. She had hinted before at the effectiveness of such treatments for my uncle's condition.

Around midnight, we still hadn't slept, sitting in the living room talking about random things when my aunt called me into her room. After closing the door, she asked me to sit down and said:

'I don't think you're unaware of your father's condition.'

I couldn't lie to her, so I replied:

'I know. The doctor told me.'

She was silent for a while, and it was hard to tell what she was thinking. Then she said:

'Anyway, I've spent the past two days searching for a remedy that might help him. I travelled to a woman up north... They say she's saved many people from death.'

'And did you come back with the remedy?'

'No, not at all. She wants a lot of money... I don't know where we'll get it from!'

'How much exactly? We have the money.'

I said this despite my doubts about my aunt's plan and my distrust of these charlatans. I knew it was all a scam. I could have told her that, according to the doctors, my uncle's recovery was unlikely, and that all we could do was be patient and pray for him. Anything else is just falsehood and a waste of time and money. But she wouldn't have believed me. She might have even suspected that I didn't want her husband to recover, thinking that greed had taken hold of me.

'A lot... far too much, my dear.'

She named a figure so large it exceeded what we earned in a whole year from the old shop. I almost told her it was ridiculous, a blatant scam. But I held back, and she noticed the change in my expression, saying:

'I know the amount surprises you, but it's either we lose the money or your father.'

She was deeply convinced of what she was saying, and there was no point in trying to dissuade her. She wouldn't easily back down from something she believed in. I asked her:

'Did this woman mention what kind of treatment she would give?'

'No, she refused to explain anything until the money was paid. After that, she said she would come in person to oversee the treatment and stay for several days until the cure is achieved. If she were a fraud, as you seem to think, she would've just given us the remedy and explained how to use it. But she insists on coming herself. I know you and your father don't believe in these things.'

I didn't respond. If my uncle were in his right mind and consulted, he would have rejected the idea outright, as he didn't believe in such things. I replied:

'It's not about these details. We'll do whatever it takes to help him recover, but…'

She interrupted me calmly:

'The money. I know we don't have that much. Even if we sold one of the shops, At least we'd have one left.'

After thinking for a moment, I told her:

'I have a solution, but it won't work now. I could have mortgaged the shops to a politician for a loan, with an agreement to repay it later. I know some who would've helped us… at least, I think they would. But the situation in the country now has complicated everything. We don't know who will stay and who will go. No one's offering help in these circumstances.'

Indeed, the timing was difficult, and in such situations, all solutions become hard. Even the banks had issued strict measures from the first day, with limits on how much money individuals could withdraw.

The only option left was to sell the house, a solution my aunt had proposed. We had no other choice but to find a buyer as quickly as possible and move to a rented apartment until fate decided what would happen.

My aunt and I agreed that this was our last option. She urged me to start looking for a buyer right away. An idea crossed my mind, so I asked:

'Would she accept the house directly?'

My aunt smiled despite her stress and worry, replying:

'I know you are intelligent, I thought of that and suggested it to her, but she refused. She only wants cash.'

'Then I'll have to think about selling it.'

For two days, I did everything I could to sell the house, but my efforts failed. No one had enough money due to the restrictions imposed by the new government and the limits on bank withdrawals. Moreover, one of the woman's conditions was that she would not accept a check; she wanted physical cash to count and verify before starting the treatment.

Although I found two potential buyers, none had the money to meet her demands. Two of our customers and my uncle's respectable friends wanted to buy, unaware of the reason behind the sale. Had they known, they might have objected, as there were still kind-hearted people around. I know they think the same way of my uncle and won't accept this obvious blackmail, but what can I do with my aunt, there's no way to convince her.

My cousin had sensed that something was going on, although I hadn't told her anything, as per my aunt's request. She noticed my long absences from the house, even though work had almost stopped due to the extended curfew hours. She must have also seen that my expressions weren't quite right, as if I seemed sad or frustrated while trying to keep myself together.

This was true regarding my state of mind and the inner conflict I felt between wanting to cure my uncle, if possible, and my aunt's obsessive desire to sell the house.

On the second evening, I told my aunt:

'There's no solution in sight. I don't know what to do.'

She looked at me, upset, and said angrily:

'Your father is dying, and you don't know how to come up with the money to save him. Where is all that praise about you being a genius?'

I wouldn't have been angry with her; I know she acts and speaks out of the pain and helplessness she is experiencing, and I too feel helpless.

There is no solution for me except for a heavenly miracle, as they say. Miracles can happen, even if only once in a lifetime, as my uncle says sometimes. At such a moment, all problems are resolved, and one feels that the law of fate is stronger than all human reasoning and people's determination to find solutions in hasty logical ways.

Once, a miracle happened when my old friend came and got me out of prison, and then disappeared. But this time, nothing seems to be looming on the horizon. Nevertheless, my heart whispered that a solution was coming. Something had to happen. That strange devil that occasionally pops up in the brain told me, even if that solution was death, uncle's end.

I sought forgiveness from my Lord and said to myself, 'What is this bad habit that haunts me? How can I control that unknown place within me that triggers some disturbing thoughts? Does this happen to everyone?' I think so. Otherwise, how could some good people suddenly turn into evil ones without any apparent reason or logical justification?

I was feeling distressed, and there was no clear idea in my mind of what to do. I decided to pray a few rak'ahs hoping that Allah might help me reach a resolution with this matter.

Indeed, I went to the mosque near the house. It was not a specific prayer time, but the mosque doors were always open, where many people find a place to spend the night and sleep under the fans hanging from the high ceiling.

As soon as I performed ablution, I began a deep prayer. I think I prayed for a long time without noticing; my need for Allah's help led me into this engrossment where I was unaware of what exactly I was doing.

Between my bowing and prostration, while one of the mosque attendees lowered the lighting by turning off some of the lamps, it seemed to me that I saw a figure moving in front of me near the window by which I was praying. Did I see it or not? I'm not entirely sure.

Of course, I didn't interrupt my prayer, and as soon as I finished the second rak'ah, I rushed outside to catch a glimpse of the figure that had retreated down the street and vanished into the darkness, making it difficult to follow. It was my old friend, the elderly man appearing again. I started searching around, wondering if he had left something specific for me, perhaps a bag or a satchel filled with money.

It was all just illusions; there was no bag, no satchel, no money. I returned home with the image firmly in my mind, and a pleasant feeling overwhelmed me that relief was near as I was hopeful about the appearance of my friend.

As I looked at my uncle, who was in his nap, coughing softly. The man with the earring saw me. He was sitting in the living room reading. For the first time, I saw him holding a book, it was one of his wife's books, who seemed to have gone to bed early.

He asked me to sit with him for a while, and he began reading passages from the book aloud. I didn't pay much attention, being preoccupied with my own concerns and the story of the old man and the imaginary money I was supposed to have received. He noticed that I wasn't paying attention and put the book aside, upside down, without closing it. He asked me:

'What's wrong? Are you still angry with me?'

'No, I'm not angry at all... just there's something on my mind... a small problem I'm trying to solve.'

Of course, I couldn't explain or clarify the nature of what troubled me. But he looked at me intensely and said after a short pause, as if he was thinking about something:

'Most of the world's problems are caused by money. Is your problem related to money?'

I didn't answer, maintaining my silence. I heard him repeat the question again, while my aunt had arrived—where from, and where she had been, I didn't focus.

She was standing in front of us, and had probably heard part of our conversation. She was still tense and angry, unable to control her emotions, reminding me of the days following the shop closure due to the murder committed by the fat man, and her frustration with me back then because I was a stranger.

She confronted the earring man, nearly grabbing his lower jaw, saying:

'Do you have a solution, you effeminate one? It's about money... yes, nothing else...'

The earring man stood up, surprised to see the lady in front of him, also he was surprised by her description of him. He did not expect this, as evident from his embarrassed expression, unlike his usual demeanour. He replied politely to my aunt:

'I can help with the matter... how much is needed exactly brother?'

My aunt, growing more agitated, replied:

'Help? I'm the one asking, not him.'

He responded, appearing as a trustworthy man contrary to his previous image in our minds:

'It makes no difference to me. I'm part of the family... isn't that right?'

My aunt felt a bit embarrassed. she stepped back and replied:

'Sorry, my son... I'm exhausted and tired... the issue concerns your uncle; we must do something for him. That's the whole problem. We didn't want to worry you. We know that money is hard to come by these days… life is no longer easy as it used to be.'

He revealed a smile showing a golden tooth that I noticed for the first time, and said to my aunt:

'Life was never easy, Aunt… it is just like this.'

He came over to me, took me aside after asking my aunt for permission, and asked me to clarify what exactly was needed. I had no choice but to tell him, as my aunt had already revealed it.

I told him the whole story honestly, without holding anything back. I expected his reaction to be resistant to the solution my aunt suggested, and that he would describe it as clear fraud. However, he reacted completely differently and said:

'Sometimes these solutions are better… I know great sultans in Turkey's history who were treated with simple methods that one wouldn't have thought of.'

I wanted to explain to him, and he had already understood my intention, so he interrupted me, adding seriously:

'Tell me, how much do you need exactly?'

I told him the amount, and his reaction was surprising to me. The amount seemed quite ordinary to him, as I saw. He said:

'In two days, I will arrange the amount for you… I will travel to Turkey and return.'

I told my aunt, and while she was almost overjoyed to the point of madness, she was also extremely surprised by the man's behaviour. She said to me:

'I didn't think he was valuable… my assessment of him was wrong.'

I didn't comment, just gave her a kiss on the cheek. I saw her crying tears of joy as she ran through the living room and then to the courtyard searching for the earring man to embrace him tightly and wail aloud, saying:

'My son… sorry, my son… I never meant to insult you.'

The night passed quickly towards dawn, and the man with earring lay on the couch in the living room, struggling against sleep, the book falling from him, then he picked it up, and so on until he finally succumbed to sleep.

I watched him, reflecting on how I hadn't appreciated him properly at first, and at the same time, I felt sympathy for his condition, especially after hearing about his nervous illness from his wife.

As he fell into a deep sleep, he began uttering his usual curses towards my uncle, and this time added my aunt to the list.

She heard the insults from afar and laughed, as the important thing was that when the man was awake, he was kind. Strangely, that evening, I didn't see him smoke at all, which was not his habit—perhaps because he was not drunk.

7
In facing the ruthless hawk

These are the mysterious divine fates. No one, my son, can understand what is happening today, nor what will happen tomorrow. No one understands how life deals with us.

The man with the earring had kept his promise and travelled at noon to Turkey. His wife knew about it from him and seemed happy that he would help us be happy, even though she wasn't convinced by my aunt's idea.

She discussed it with me as a scam, but she believed that as long as there was hope, one had to pursue it. A person must try even things that seem pointless. And soon, a day would be passed and another to reveal what fate had hidden for us to happen.

The next morning, I had gone out to the new shop, thinking about the wealth of the man with the earring. His wife had said that he came from a family worth millions upon millions, where gold was like dirt to them.

I thought about the irony, the measure of toil and success in life. My uncle and I had worked for many long years, thinking we were wealthy, only to face a simple situation that showed us how powerless we were in the face of numbers... human greed. The truly rich can face those numbers... they can do anything.

How do these people create such wealth? That question consumed me. What could they possibly do other than work and work? But then I remembered that the limping man once told me that immense wealth doesn't come from daily struggle but through other means, which most people can't pursue—either out of fear or because they have a conscience.

The only thing wealth requires is to kill your heart and proceed without it. Forget everything but yourself.

The man with the earring disappeared. I thought he would be gone for two days and return. He wasn't late. He had sent someone before him to bring the money. The man had arrived at the airport at night, as we learned later, carrying a bag stuffed with dollars.

There was some mistake or a deception committed by fate against this stranger visiting Sudan for the first time. And there was another arrangement—I didn't know if it was intentional or not—that the man with the earring should be delayed so he wouldn't fall into the trap, be caught by the economic security officers who had been multiplying in recent days.

The new government had imposed numerous restrictions on the movement of money, and no one expected that the situation would escalate to executions of innocent people, sometimes just middlemen or currency traders, simply because a decree was issued by a man called the President's Assistant, stating that any foreign currency harms the national economy and its holder is to be punished by death. That was the law and the Shariah, under which many were thrown into prison, with no escape once the trap was sprung.

My aunt believed that the man with the earring was a fraud, and that's why he was delayed. Perhaps he reached his country and realised the value of the money and gold and decided not to return, or he forgot about the matter. But his wife never doubted him, saying:

'I've never known him to lie when he made a promise or committed to something.'

My aunt was in her most desperate state, at her wit's end. She spoke loudly, saying:

'I knew he was a fraud... He wanted to run away.'

Run away? From what and why? She couldn't provide any explanation or clarify anything to anyone. She just made judgments, having lost her reason in the face of my uncle's deteriorating condition and her great faith that the only solution would come through the charlatan waiting for money to rise and heal my uncle.

I knew it was a scam and waited for the man with the earring to return to solve the problem, as I was overwhelmed by an inexplicable feeling that the man was not lying.

We stayed in this state of waiting until we received the news after ten days. An investigator in civilian clothes arrived at the new shop, presenting his badge as an economic security officer, saying he had come to investigate me. When I asked why, he replied:

'You'll find out everything when you reach our office.'

I sat in a small office with only one chair, an old wooden table, and three men who spat frequently on the ground, all in civilian clothes. One of them wore dark sunglasses, and I had a vague feeling that I'd seen him before, perhaps during one of those past times when I was arrested during the church raid. And my suspicion wasn't wrong this time, as the man spoke to me:

'O Christian… Did you think they would do you any good? They use you, then discard you. They all play this role.'

Without any introduction, he jumped straight to the point, as if we'd spoken before. Then he said:

'It doesn't matter whether you know me or remember me… because now you've become important.'

He laughed loudly, inappropriately, and then walked toward the door, knocking on it and calling for another man:

'Come deal with this lame hunchback.'

Once again, I found myself confronting my deformity. Now I had two deformities. This is my fate. I remained silent, having developed the ability to endure and face such people with silence. They were filled with hatred, envy, and all the ugly tumours of the world's misfortunes. They were reflections of a corrupt era, as my aunt had described them when she later heard the story from me. The investigator asked me:

'What are you going to do with those millions?'

'What millions?'

'Don't pretend you don't understand. We understand.'

'You may understand, but I don't.'

The man approached to slap me, while the one with the dark glasses was laughing and rubbing his penis that was boiling. These people had no shame. Of course, I didn't tell my aunt this part, as I focused on narrating the rest of what had happened.

The important thing was that I learned the matter concerned the man with the earring. specifically, the poor man who became the victim. He is now imprisoned in a distant jail reserved for the so-called 'dollar mafia'.

I was told the money had been confiscated with no chance of recovery and that a verdict would be issued in two days by a special court inside the prison. The likely sentence is death—there's no lesser punishment to expect. These are the orders of the senior assistant.

'But this man is innocent.'

I said, only to hear the man in the black sunglasses continue with his malice, saying:

'They all say that... they're all innocent.'

'But this will cause problems with another country. He's not a citizen,' I interrupted.

The man with the sunglasses laughed as he replied:

'The ruthless hawk doesn't want our country to rely on anyone else. Didn't you hear his speech yesterday? Alone, we are capable of building this country from scratch... haha... hahahaha... haaa.'

Those laughs still haunt me at night when I can't sleep, while my aunt paces the hallway back and forth, eventually reaching the outer gate as the wind howls violently, battering the windows and doors as if the apocalypse were upon us.

My cousin had secluded herself in a far-off room three days ago and rarely emerged, as if she were writing something—I often saw her sharpening pencils. She only writes in pencil, as she once told me. Meanwhile, my uncle remained in his isolation.

Before the verdict was issued, or we learned of its content, the man with the earring had returned. He arrived the night following my interrogation. He arrived when the weather was terrible, with thick dust storms and scattered, powerless rain unable to quell the raging dust.

My aunt, in her usual stride, reached the outer door to find him standing before her. She grabbed him. I watched them from afar, unable to discern the nature of their encounter as she embraced him. Was she happy he was back? Was she exacting revenge for the lost money?

Everything was so dreadful that it was hard to find explanations for people's behaviour s under such circumstances. Sometimes we struggle to understand what's happening around us and the actions of others, even if we've lived among them for decades. Human nature is very complex—this is my life lesson, not one inherited from my uncle.

I heard her tell him what had happened. I couldn't make out the exact words, but I gathered from their actions what was said—this was a skill I occasionally possessed, though not always. At other times, my mind would simply go numb.

I saw him appear troubled, collapsing on my aunt's shoulder as though he were crying or performing some act I couldn't fully interpret, though it seemed to involve confusion and sorrow, mixed with a desire for revenge.

He didn't enter the house to greet me or see his wife. Instead, he slammed the outer door and disappeared. My aunt returned inside and told me:

'He now knows his brother is facing death.'

'His brother...!'

I hadn't known that before, and I wasn't supposed to know. The interrogators only take statements; they don't provide information, aside from the grim news of death and executions.

My cousin had come out of her room, sensing something unusual, and she understood that her husband had returned and that the man currently imprisoned was her husband's brother. She didn't seem particularly interested in the rest of the story, as if it didn't concern her.

I had no reason to talk to her; I didn't understand why her mood had changed so much in the past days. Was it the absence of the man with the earring, or was it her deep focus on writing—that mysterious craft I knew nothing about?

That fateful, harsh evening, if I may call it that, filled me with pain and longing as I recall it now. I remember my uncle's image. On that night, fate, woven into the threads of the unseen, spread wings of terror over the great city, as if a mighty angel had descended from the heavens to declare the end of days.

I heard a towering voice come from a distant place—at least, I heard it. It came from the room where my uncle lay, calling out with all the strength he could muster.

His booming voice bore no trace of illness—none of the rare rasp or the burdens of these hard days that had weakened his body. I stood before him, my aunt behind me, and my cousin behind her. He stood like a horse defeated in battle, ready to deliver his final speech before departure.

He pulled me to him with surprising strength, embracing my frail body. I saw him stronger than I had ever seen him before—as though he could lift a mountain. With his other hand, he pulled his daughter close and embraced her too. He told us:

'Be one hand.'

And then, he was gone, swallowed by the strange unknown.

The dazzling power that had surged through him gradually faded, as he gazed at my aunt with an overwhelming affection, speaking to her in the silent language of the eyes. She understood what he meant, and the light of his spirit dimmed, leaving behind a smile that still lingers in this house to this day, my son. I can almost feel it walking through every corner of this house.

This is your grandfather's house. It shaped my world and my life, my son. This is the house that could have been lost had we sold it, and with it, the memories of those days and years would have disappeared too.

Life moves forward with all its events and happenings, leaving us, in the end, with only fleeting glimpses of memories that we must cling to, to feel a touch of happiness in our weary souls in this existence.

What is suffering, my son, except the feeling of alienation and the absence of memories in a place? A stranger tries to ease his loneliness by searching for a ghost in the night—a ghost of an old memory that once dwelled here.

It was my uncle's will, written years ago, which my aunt retrieved from the large cabinet in the house, to be buried here in the country he loved and made his refuge.

I later discovered that my uncle possessed a beautiful, adorned language in his writing, something I never knew before. I thought to myself, perhaps this is the secret behind my sister becoming a writer. I had the ability to distinguish well-written words that were filled with love and sincerity.

My aunt informed us, me and the men around me, that we needed to prepare the grave in the large cemetery not far from our house and before the new dawn arrived, the house had filled with mourners. How they knew the news, how they managed to defy the darkness and the rain that had started to fall, and how they reached us after the fierce storms of the night subsided, I do not know.

It wasn't the time to look for answers. Despite everything, despite the harshness of the new regime in the country, despite the army's armored vehicles still in the streets and on the bridges, despite the violence and deception, the people did their duty perfectly. They dug the grave, prepared the funeral, and scattered perfume on the ground, which mixed with the scent of rain-soaked earth, reminding me of the image of my father, daring the rainy night to enter the house drunk and start beating my mother.

I erased that last image from my mind to focus on the image of my old father, a creature deserving of pity, struggling against old childhood wounds—perhaps in moments I do not understand or have forgotten.

I wept bitterly, unsure if my tears were for my old father or my new father, for the years that had passed while I lived in a world between dream and reality with the family that loved me.

My cousin hugged me tightly, crying. The only person absent from this scene was the man with the earring—no one knew where he had gone.

My father (my uncle) used to say that this people, despite the profound tragedy and pain that has begun to drive its nails into their backs, will one day be able to triumph over its sufferings. That's why he loves this land.

This was part of a lengthy will that included other matters, such as the story of the deed in my name and my inheritance of almost half of his estate, along with the matter of taking care of my aunt and that I should treat her like a true mother and allow her the freedom to live here or there.

My uncle had commented while sketching smiling faces next to his notes in the will. I don't think she will leave me to return to the land of our ancestors, but if you think for a moment, you'll find that many ancestors were buried beneath this land a century ago. He was referring specifically to the Turks who ruled Sudan in the 19th century.

The burial ceremonies ended; my aunt was very steadfast and strong. I never saw her defeated by the death of her husband. She was brave enough to earn everyone's respect, even though some women viewed her as unfortunate for not knowing how to cry for her companion properly. Some women think this way; a woman must shed a lot of tears and wail loudly to be said to have loved her husband.

I was certain of the love that resided in her heart, and I knew that my aunt was a person who lived life as she wanted it, in the way she desired to appear, even if at times she indulged in fanciful and illogical matters. Yet I would say that each of us has our flaws, mistakes, and stumbles; no one is perfect in this world. That was also my uncle's wisdom.

Two days after my uncle's death, the man with the earring had not shown up, which became a personal concern for me, especially when my sister urged me to do something, saying:

'He can't be gone for this long… maybe something happened to him.'

It all started from that place where I had been interrogated… no one else. But before I could take any action, I found I didn't have enough time, as the mourners did not cease to come.

The fat man had arrived, and he had regained his health despite his old age. How did he learn the news and where had he been? It wasn't the right time to ask; I welcomed him, and

I couldn't hold back my tears, as we found ourselves crying together.

He cried with deep anguish, raising his voice in pleas to unknown beings to preserve my uncle's legacy, and in between each plea, he would embrace me and continue his wailing.

He asked to meet my aunt to console her, and he did. He knelt in the dirt before her, sincere in every detail of his actions. Then he took my leave and departed without solving the mystery regarding him. As days passed, I found that I would forget, as I usually do, and not retain details for long.

After he left, in the midday sun, I had to do something about the man with the earring. One of our major clients, who was dealing with us, came to offer condolences and apologised for being late, claiming he had been travelling. I knew he worked in those secret areas of the security forces, but where? I wasn't sure.

I had to enlist someone's help; I took him aside and recounted the story to him. He said:

'They are wicked people who can do anything.'

'What do you mean... that his brother could die?'

'Both could face any fate. I know my people well, but let me try to take action.'

I didn't trust his reaction or his willingness to help, but what could I do but take some kind of action?

I told him about my interrogation and the other details from two nights ago, and he urged me to wait until evening and not to approach anyone else.

I remained in a state of uncertainty, welcoming more mourners, most of whom were friends of my uncle, and a representative from the Turkish community attended with the ambassador, who delivered a speech about the strong relations between the two countries. He was accompanied by a group of young men with cameras and video equipment, and the next day, these images made it to the press.

As I was bidding farewell to the ambassador and his entourage, it occurred to me to inform him about what had happened, as this matter could turn political, and any uncalculated action would have negative repercussions on the strong relations the diplomat spoke of.

Just as I was supposed to speak, even though I had promised that man, the man with the earring appeared from a distance, bringing with him a man who looked just like him, even with the same dangling earring; it was undoubtedly his brother. I had been interrogated, but I hadn't been allowed to see him.

He was smiling as if his money had been returned to him and told me that the matter had been resolved but he hadn't received the funds. He said:

'What's important is that my brother has escaped the noose... this ruthless hawk can do anything to gather money and maintain power.'

Although it wasn't the right time to show signs of laughter, I couldn't help but respond:

'You were elated the day the man appeared on television as if you were his minister'

He showed no interest in my comment and continued:

'Your friend is a high-ranking official... he took care of everything... without him, the issue wouldn't have been resolved... what position does he hold?'

I had no idea; all I knew was that he was one of the secretive men of authority. I told him:

'I don't know anything about him...'

The man with the earring asked, uninterested in hearing any further details about his brother:

'What was the ambassador doing here?'

'Do you know he's the ambassador?'

'I know him well; he's a big opportunist... he was a candidate in our district back in Turkey... and he won after pouring everything he had to win the election.'

I myself was surprised by the ambassador's presence; my uncle had no connections in these circles throughout his life, maintaining only relationships within his daily work environment. He rarely associated with people from his homeland. Did the ambassador come because of the man with the earring?

Perhaps that was true. I imagined that when the ambassador saw the man with the earring approaching us, he recognised him and tried to step forward to greet him, but the man with the earring seemed to avoid him, or he avoided him altogether and didn't step towards him until the ambassador had to leave.

I told myself that these were just fantasies in my mind, and I dismissed the matter from my thoughts. I turned to arrange the ordinary affairs of life.

The next morning, the newspapers were published as usual, featuring pictures of the Turkish ambassador, in which I appeared with my tall unkempt hair, wearing a long cap and an open shirt. I had never worn the traditional jilbab and turban. Beneath the photo, it was written, 'Son of the late...' and also in bold letters, 'A Turkish family that loves this country and its people... and builds its glory within it'.

No one could easily recognised me, not even my relatives or close friends. I had no friends aside from my family and my work.

Overnight, I became part of the creators of glory in this country because of a picture. Many approached me afterward, asking cautiously, 'Are you that young Turkish man whose pictures were published in the newspapers? Are you the son of the Turkish millionaire who loved our country and insisted on being buried here?' One of them said to me, 'Do you know that hundreds of us die abroad and are brought back in coffins? Your father truly loved this land. Thank him for us.'

A journalist came to the shop days later, saying he wanted to interview me to create an exclusive piece, urging the youth to stop migrating abroad because this country has opportunities for those who want to succeed. 'Look, Turks are thriving here,' he said, while every young person thinks their salvation lies overseas.

I completely rejected the idea of the interview, shutting the door on anyone who thought they could exploit my uncle's story to promote a false nationalism in the media. I had begun to understand that those who talk about this country and its growth are often the same ones working to destroy it and stifle its talents.

Days passed, and soon the country was at war again. The forests in the south were ablaze, and the ruthless hawk sent the youth into its raging volcanoes to die mercilessly in the name of God and the Prophet and that lie called nationalism.

Life became difficult after my uncle's death. I found that he had created a real void in my life and that he was indeed the only person in this world I loved sincerely more than anyone else—more than those whom laws and customs call family.

I would remember him and start to cry, unable to control myself. My aunt, too, could not believe it; all her strength and resilience she had shown to the mourners had vanished. Now, faced with solitude, she had no choice but to confront the past, memories, and longing.

She imagined he hadn't died, speaking to him in the hallways of the house and in the courtyard, entering his room and I could hear her having long conversations with him, telling him:

'Our son is coming. He hasn't died.'

She meant her old son but would sometimes mix it up, holding me and saying to my uncle, whom she imagined was present:

'Here is our son... He has come... Can you hear him?'

She asked me to greet him and kiss him on the forehead, and I did so into the empty void, while she felt joy at what was happening.

This happened while the house had emptied of everyone except me and her. The daughter had left with her husband; they stayed only a week after the death. The daughter was sad but calmly said:

'What can we do? It's fate.'

I saw her as a believer, strong in facing it. As for the man with the earring, although I thought I understood this character for some time, that was impossible; he seemed eccentric once again. He grabbed a long hair from his brother's head, pulling it hard as they left, cursing him for wasting their money. Then he looked at me, saying:

'He is the cause of this trouble; he is our real thief.'

I paid no attention to what I heard, as they were travelling anyway.

Time was moving slowly as if its rules had changed. I thought that sometimes when we lose people we love, life makes us confused about everything. We can't understand things or live by the beliefs we once had. This really happens. But as days pass, life starts to shine again, and we find ourselves falling into another illusion—that we are immortal and must keep living, creating a false version of ourselves in this world.

So, after several months, I had to return to being that persevering young man who reads self-help books and success skills, then works hard as much as he can, moving between the new and old shop, after I had changed many details and hung my uncle's picture at the entrance of both shops, as a symbol of the struggle I had to continue in his path.

I faced numerous difficulties at work after about a year, as the state imposed exorbitant taxes on trade in all its forms, even selling refreshments on the streets for those suffering from the extreme heat during the day. Everyone was pursued by authorities to pay money collected for one goal: war.

Day by day, we heard that dozens of soldiers had been wiped out entirely, but the truths had no place on the ground. It's hard to understand what's actually happening. I didn't care about that.

I knew that politics affected my work, and I was forced to solve my problems related to this complex side by doing what I had long believed I would never resort to: paying bribes to tax men, municipal contractors, and licensing, health, and sanitation officials.

I reached the conclusion that to survive, I had to do this, as the country was sinking lower and lower in values. Was yesterday really like this, or was I too young to comprehend? I remember my uncle once told me:

'Life is as it is; it doesn't change. People behave the same way throughout time. But one doesn't truly understand things until one's awareness has fully matured.'

So today I have truly grown. Many things and convictions have grown with me, along with a stubbornness to forget the distant past completely. I… I am not someone else; I am the one who loves himself as he loves himself, not as others want him to. A person is himself and nothing else. I cared only for myself and my aunt, for some mysterious reason that drew me to her, perhaps that feeling of motherhood stolen from me, the same feeling that filled me towards my late uncle.

She, too, had to adapt over time to the reality that I was the only one who cared about her in this world. She had no beloved, no friend, no relative… and no mention of family lost in oblivion. She had also been forced, whether due to awareness or perhaps the curse of life and its cruelty when it insists on confirming its things, to realize that my uncle had died.

One evening, she took me to the cemetery and placed wreaths of flowers on the grave, a rare ritual in our culture. No one in our country brings flowers to the dead, which is why our presence in the cemetery seemed strange to those who saw us, leaving them puzzled about what was happening.

As we were returning home in the car I had bought just weeks ago, which I was driving myself as part of the new rules of my life, it occurred to me to ask my aunt about her family. Where are they? About her past? About my uncle's past? I said to her:

'There are so many stories my uncle was supposed to tell me before he died, but…'

She interrupted me while gazing into the empty night around us. I think she was trying to sense whether the moon was in the sky or not. She said:

'History has no meaning unless it has an impact on our present…'

I had never known her to be wise like my uncle, but today, she seemed filled with rare wisdom. Life shapes a person many times over, making them see what they couldn't grasp just yesterday, or even moments ago.

I understood then that she didn't want to talk about her childhood memories or how her relationship with my uncle had developed, or even if it existed at all. She doesn't like recalling anything about Turkey, whether good or bad. Does she have dark memories there? A painful past?

I was too shy to ask, and she clearly didn't want to talk about it. But maybe the right moment would come, if the question really mattered and needed to be asked again, as she hinted.

Days passed after visiting the cemetery, and I started dreaming at night that I was travelling to Turkey and marrying my cousin after her husband, the man with the earring, died—or rather, I had killed him. He seemed evil and fierce, and I had to get rid of him to win my love.

In the dream, I loved my cousin deeply and felt I had to marry her by any means necessary. Of course, dreams lack logic, and I acted on my overwhelming feelings of love.

Upon waking, I was puzzled by the nature of the relationship I had with my cousin, whom I called my sister. Did I really love her? What made her fill my heart, causing such a strong fluttering sensation throughout my body whenever I pictured her? Sometimes, this even happened at work, to the point where one of the workers noticed and jokingly remarked, which was rare for me at work:

'Have you found something to fill your inner void, sir?'

I smiled at him with a warning not to make such silly jokes again and to focus on his duties. He understood I was being serious, knowing I appreciated those who worked hard with me and that I was always generous with them.

These moments would pass, and I would forget her entirely, only to remember again later. After the dreams stopped, I rarely thought of her, except during those quiet nighttime hours before falling asleep, imagining her sitting across from me in the living room during the days she spent with us. Sometimes I would even imagine her holding and kissing me, and in other moments, I pictured her naked in my waking thoughts.

This remained my state until one day, while I was sitting in the shop, which had since grown old, a mature woman—a young, strong, and bold one—stood in front of me. I recognised her immediately by her dark complexion her vibrantly embroidered clothing, though she had aged slightly. Or perhaps life had simply moved forward, and we only notice it suddenly when we pause.

I quickly reached out to shake her hand. She sat on a high chair near the wall, looking around the shop, and asked me:

'Is this yours?'

'Yes, it is mine,' I replied.

'I've thought about you often, and I was sure you'd become important someday,' she said seriously.

'Just a shawarma shop. Is this the importance you see in a man?' I responded with brief sarcasm.

'Your father, the priest, used to say your problem was that you don't take anything seriously,' she replied seriously.

This was hard for me to accept, as I believed I was very serious. Yet here she was, saying the opposite. Does seriousness mean handling things with a mix of chaos and firmness? Is that what I lack—the ability to create chaos in my life, to laugh, to stay up late with friends, to drink alcohol, or at least smoke a cigarette?

She observed me as I noticed something unusual in her face. Tiny black dots, as if delicately drawn by a sharp tool, had appeared on her forehead. They hadn't been there before, and I wanted to ask her about them. But it seemed like such a question would be inappropriate, so instead, I asked:

'Where have you been all these years?'

'I went to America to finish my studies in political science, with direct support from the commander of the Liberation Army.'

She replied, glancing at me to emphasize that she had also become important. She waved her finger to show me a stunning gold engagement ring, and for the first time since she had entered the shop, she softened a bit, saying:

'I asked about you a lot until I found you here. I always felt something drawing me to you since those days, but life doesn't always follow one's will.'

There was a sadness in her, one that resembled the look on my Turkish cousin's face at times. Perhaps they shared some resemblance, formed in my mind and influenced by my mood—a resemblance others might not see.

I felt my heart race, mixed with fear. Maybe it was true that I hadn't thought about her since the day I entered the church and started working with the priest, thanks to her introducing me to him. Yet today, as she stood before me after rising from the long chair and adjusting her skirt, straightening her chain that ended in a small cross, she planted a mysterious seed in an unclear part of my soul. Life, like this moment, felt like a dream.

Was she that girl who caught my attention in those distant mornings when I was wandering aimlessly? I wasn't sure. Sometimes, we don't fully grasp what happened just yesterday.

I wanted to understand how she found me, or why she spent time searching for me, and what she wanted from me.

These questions seemed selfish and unimportant. What mattered was that she cared about me, and that was enough. Now, I realize that at least, I am happy with her. I told her:

'Whatever happens, please don't disappear from my life.'

She responded with a sorrowful expression, which I could read on her face, and said:

'Sometimes, there are things we can only do once. We may not meet again. Tomorrow at dawn, I'm flying to Nairobi. There are many things waiting for me. We have long and ongoing battles. I don't know when the war will end, so I can have a little time to think about myself.'

'Aren't you afraid they'll catch you if they find out you were here?' I asked her.

She revealed perfectly aligned white teeth held together by a metallic brace as she replied:

'No one but you know that I am in the north. If anything happens, that means it's you.'

She laughed unexpectedly, then suddenly kissed me on the cheek, making me feel embarrassed in front of the other customers.

She fled, disappearing into the crowd on the street. I saw nothing as I removed my glasses, and everything blurred before my eyes. When I put them back on, I saw nothing but a sea of cars and people rushing toward their fates.

Things were difficult for everyone. The external grip on the country was tightening as it was classified on the international terrorism list. There were rumours that a prominent religious leader had settled here after leaving Afghanistan, which would undoubtedly complicate matters further.

Some men sitting in the shop whispered about these things while eating, fearing that someone might overhear them. They added:

'But maybe the Sheikh's wealth will ease the situation. They say he has a lot of money.'

Years passed, and the dark-skinned girl from the south never returned. It seemed she became busy with the war and preparing for peace negotiations that everyone was talking about, especially after the oil started flowing from the southern fields. This slightly improved the economy, though the general hardship didn't end, and a new war ignited in the west of the country.

I stayed focused on my path and my vow to build my success. My uncle's advice to devote myself entirely to work was ever-present.

My aunt became a great support, finally coming to the realization that life must go on. She would often visit the old shop near the house, managing the accounts there, while I focused on the new shop. We doubled the number of workers after business improved, and the number of customers grew, especially with the return of soldiers who were the biggest fans of shawarma.

As usual, when I immerse myself in work, I forget everything else. Days passed in this routine of work. At night, my aunt and I would sit for an hour, organizing the next day's affairs, reviewing the accounts, and then resting, ready for the new day.

My car helped a lot with my mobility until I decided, with my aunt's approval, to open two more shops. One was inside a military base after I won a big tender for which I had invested a lot of time and money. It wasn't an easy task, but I was confident it would be mine.

The second shop was in a new residential area east of the Blue Nile, where the state had built a new bridge, expanding residential neighbourhoods in that direction. I didn't know why I chose that area, but I often let my heart guide me in some decisions. My aunt, when I told her the idea, said that the location was one that no one else would think of.

I felt like I was no longer just learning; I was now implementing and applying the accumulated knowledge I had gained over the years, both from my uncle and my own efforts. Through daily struggles with people and life, I often wondered when I saw young men wandering the streets with no jobs or purpose: why don't they work? Why don't they fight for a better tomorrow? My uncle used to say, 'This country is full of gold, but no one sees it.'

For me, I always thought that if I had finished my education—which seemed impossible in my earlier circumstances—and graduated from university, would I be one of those aimless drifters on the streets? It's a miracle to create value for yourself in this place, given the harsh conditions and the dominance of certain people over everything.

Life felt like a predetermined path that I was following, or perhaps I had already been walking this path without even realizing it.

A few months after the peace agreement was signed and the fighters returned from the south, I found myself increasingly occupied with never-ending work, especially at the military base, which consumed most of the expenses but also generated the highest revenue.

During those long, busy days, the thought occasionally crossed my mind that the elegant dark-skinned girl might return since everyone else had come back. But I never heard from her or saw her again. Instead, I received bad news about my old friend, the shoeshine boy who once shared a room with me. The room had since been replaced by a seven-story building owned by a military officer. It seemed that in the final days, everything had come under military control, leaving civilians like my uncle completely sidelined. I had not heard anything about him or his family for a long time.

It was a terrible day when a young man, one of the returning fighters from a nearby African country where the agreement had been signed, sat down and began telling his comrades about the horrors of war and the millions who had died there. He recounted how the armies thought only of death. My friend's name came up, and I confirmed it through their descriptions. I should have cried or felt a deep sorrow, but nothing happened.

Had I become heartless, devoid of emotions? This troubled me. Had I become hardened and emotionless? The only explanation I could give was that so much time had passed since we last met, and so the spaces in our hearts had gradually been erased. This must have been what happened to me—it was the easiest explanation so I wouldn't strip myself of my humanity.

Months passed, and as my wealth doubled and I became more skilled in bribery and seizing opportunities amidst traders, politicians, and military officers in this chaos they called 'serving the national interest' on TV, I learned to use new technologies like mobile phones, computers, and the internet to manage my business. My accounts were now handled in a modern way, as my customers often said, many of whom thought I was Turkish, the son of a Turk.

I didn't bother to correct them, whether by denying or confirming it. I carried on as before, with no need to convince anyone otherwise.

Sometimes, I even took advantage of this perception to gain benefits, as foreigners had become privileged in our country in the new century. They had sprawling businesses wherever you went. Some attributed my success to this latest trend, lumping me in with the Syrians, Gulf Arabs, Iranians, and Moroccans who had arrived in recent years and made fortunes in various sectors such as agriculture, industry, and restaurants—even private schools.

Suddenly, I discovered that, at a certain point in life, when a mysterious equation is fulfilled, money starts flowing from every direction. This is what happened to me. I didn't know how these streams of cash kept pouring into my bank account daily.

Instead of two old shops, a shop in the military base, and another in the new eastern neighbourhood, my business expanded to over ten shops in the city, all bearing the same old sign that my friend had painted. That street boy had found his way in life through a shawarma shop.

I even bought a piece of land in the city center near the grand bank, which I had once admired for its strange and massive structure. Within months, a towering building had risen. Reinforced concrete became a new fascination in my life, and I became drawn to buildings, towers, and houses built like palaces.

I made a deal with a major company to build a luxurious house by the Blue Nile after purchasing the land from the wife of a well-known minister. She managed his private affairs, which wasn't unusual; in every previous government, it was the same—the women ran the finances and corruption, as the minister once joked when we met at his home to sign the purchase contract.

My aunt was overjoyed, and we left in my new high-end car, which I had replaced a few weeks earlier. My aunt was almost delirious with happiness and insisted we visit the construction site. The river was so close, and doves and sparrows filled the sky. Many pigeons were flying around, though we didn't know where they came from. The weather was mild, with a refreshing coolness in the air. Looking at the clear sky, I knew nothing was impossible for me.

I continued supervising the construction of my villa after the completion of the multi-story commercial building downtown.

One afternoon, an old car stopped near the construction site. A man stepped out, but I couldn't make out his features from a distance due to the dust in the air. As he approached, alongside a woman in her late thirties—average in beauty, with a pale face—I instantly recognised him as my maternal uncle. How did he know I was here?

He rushed to embrace me, unusually without his pipe. There was a profound sadness in him; he had aged much faster than I had imagined. I couldn't quite understand his pale appearance until he began to tell his story, saying painfully:

'I've come to ask for your help, and I hope you won't turn me away. Things have changed, and life has become hard because of this ruthless hawk.'

He gestured toward the woman accompanying him, who I recognised as my cousin, though she wasn't the same woman who had sat at that party one evening or the one in the old photograph.

Time had surely passed; everything in life decays with time. She had undoubtedly aged, but something else was different about both her and my uncle. I would understand it eventually, but I had to be patient.

My uncle turned to his daughter and said:

'Greet your cousin. I don't think you've met before.'

She shook my hand; her grip was firm, not reflecting the delicate appearance of a woman in jeans and a stylish white shirt with burnt edges.

I heard my uncle teasingly say to her, directing the remark toward me:

'Isn't he a handsome cute young man?'

I could guess what he was implying if I am not mistaken or deluded, as if he knew all about my affairs even though I hadn't heard from them in a long time, since the days when it was said that his daughter had taken a high-ranking administrative position in one of the ministries.

He was talking about marriage—was he here to offer his daughter to me? Then I heard her say:

'He is indeed handsome. I didn't imagine he would be this good-looking, Father.'

My uncle chuckled faintly, then pulled me aside and said:

'I have no choice but to ask for your help. I'm preparing for a major livestock trading deal, and I need to export a large quantity to the Gulf countries. No one can give me the financial loan I need except you. One of my old friends, a former minister, advised me to come to you. He told me that your nephew would help so why you go far away, as he's always been generous, and relatives are more deserving of kindness.'

I didn't think much or ask who this minister was that knew me so well. I didn't even consider whether my decision was right or wrong. That uncertainty would trouble me later. I quickly asked him how much he needed and then wrote him a check for the amount without worrying whether it was too much or too little.

Money had become a trivial game for me by then. He took the check like a child who had found his family after being lost in an amusement park, hopping around in the mud near the river, with his daughter jumping along beside him. As he drove off in his noisy old car, he said:

'Don't forget to visit us. Not at the old house, though; the government took it from us. We live in…'

He paused briefly, then said:

'I forgot to tell you that your aunt passed away about a year ago. A cruel illness took her from us… may God have mercy on her.'

I prayed for her soul, and a flood of memories of her rushed into my mind, scattered moments that were hard to piece together, especially that strange night with that vile boy, the son of the guard. I said to my uncle:

'That's the way of life. What can one do about death?'

He quickly replied, after checking once more that the check was safely in his pocket:

'It's our fate… it's all of our fates…'

Then he sped off, disappearing into the distance, leaving behind more dust in the already thick air.

I was left standing there, thinking about how quickly life can change. My uncle, who had once hosted me generously in his home, was now begging me for help. His wife, who had wielded such brutal authority over everyone, had died, and he seemed not to care much. Maybe he was sad, but neither he nor his daughter seemed to remember her fondly.

Perhaps it was just the passage of time. To be fair, I thought about myself—had I been any better? Had I done anything for my uncle, the man truly responsible for my success in life?

Since that day, many things have happened. Old faces from my past began appearing suddenly in my life. I couldn't explain how they found me or why they came back. I told myself it was the price of fame and fortune, nothing more.

This is what my aunt had told me when she insisted on burning incense and reciting her protective prayers, which she believed had the power to shield me from envy. She'd say:

'If money isn't protected, it will vanish, my boy. You must do this ritual at least once a week.'

What could I say to her? There was no way to refuse. So every morning, my aunt performed her duties, while I rushed off to my expanding business—my real estate projects and the office I had established on the seventh floor of my new building downtown.

Clients and new friends, who I had met over the years—some politicians, others football enthusiasts seeking financial support for their major clubs—would come to see me there. They even suggested I take over as president of one of the well-known clubs, insisting it would be a great honour for them and the club.

I declined, as I didn't like being in the spotlight. However, I still donated financially to the team. By doing so, I avoided interviews and media appearances. I didn't believe that a truly smart person, one who has real success, would waste time seeking public attention. On the contrary, people would seek him out.

I also received another offer from the city's Chamber of Commerce, inviting me to join them. I accepted this because I saw it as beneficial for my business. Being a member would ease many things for me, as it was important to extend your influence in places that would help you succeed.

Many people in those days doubted the continuity of the ruling regime, especially after tensions began to rise between the returnees from the war and the government, following their political partnership for power.

Some spoke of the possibility of a return to war, but the more likely scenario, as almost everyone saw it, was that the southern part of the homeland was on the path to seceding as a new country.

What mattered to me was that my affairs were going well in the country, despite the growing external blockade, including from neighbouring countries. I didn't care about the rumours circulating about me, saying I was benefiting from the new situation or that I was one of the regime's cronies, accusations promoted by some for their own purposes, some of which I understood and others I didn't.

Some said I was the regime's pampered son, and others described me as managing the president's own finances, meaning, in direct terms, that I was the agent of the ruthless hawk in his business dealings, the ones he didn't want anyone to know he was behind.

I never bothered to respond or defend myself against such talk. Matters became more complicated for me on the day I opened one of my most famous shops on the main street in the city center, near the airport, not far from my old store. Dozens of newspapers and TV channels, which had become abundant in those days, rushed to cover the event, and I was surprised to see the president himself among the attendees.

The ruthless hawk sometimes appeared at social and commercial events unannounced, perhaps just for entertainment. I was certain that the man didn't come for any of the reasons fabricated by the rumours spreading through the country, I mean he didn't come to inaugurate one of his personal investments in restaurants.

My aunt was the happiest person that day, watching the ruthless hawk cut the ribbon as gunshots rang out into the sky, accompanied by the colours of fireworks.

I felt immense joy, filled with a slight pain, wishing my uncle had been there that happy day. He would have been convinced that his investment had paid off, as he had always bet in his life that I would become something great one day.

What pleased me most was that the president, in a short speech, referred to me as an example of hardworking youth and a real model of patriotism. But what was even more important in his speech increased the suspicions of those who believed I wasn't Sudanese, but Turkish, when he said:

'I hear some say that our son is from friendly Turkey, but I say it doesn't matter where you're from… What matters is that you're a son of this country when you serve it and contribute to it.'

Later that night, after everything had settled down, my aunt asked me:

'You're something else, son. You've reached the president himself!'

I was deep in thought and replied:

'I don't know how he decided to come here… While I'm happy, I'm also wary.'

'Don't worry about it now that it's happened. The president has other things to occupy him; don't forget there's a fierce war in the west of the country. You should focus on what matters to you. As you progress in life, the path gets narrower and harder, not easier and lined with roses like people think,' she said to me.

My aunt wasn't right that the president had more pressing matters. In reality, he was a complex machine working under all circumstances and in every direction.

Just days later—though I didn't count them—a man and a woman came to my office on the seventh floor, introducing themselves as from the ruthless hawk's office, delivering a message.

I quickly opened the envelope and read the letterhead:

Presidency of the Republic
Office of the Ruthless Hawk

The message requested that I swiftly respond to the call of duty by transferring a specific amount to a designated account. I was urged not to delay, as the country had commitments, and people like me were expected to fulfill their obligations early. There was no explicit threat, but the tone of the letter, signed by the president, hinted at a veiled warning that I should immediately comply.

The two visitors said very little and quickly took their leave with great courtesy. This is how things seem at first. I learned this lesson and kept it on my mind from far away time.

I stayed in my office for an hour, contemplating. I'm neither stingy nor cowardly, but was this the point of the whole story? Did the president show up and play this role just to achieve this end?

The amount wasn't trivial; it was a direct, explicit extortion from the highest authority in the land. What was I to do? There was no law I could turn to. First, I needed to verify the situation.

I didn't contact my aunt to tell her—it would only worry her. I knew she would be overly concerned, and I rarely involved her in such matters over the years. I only put her in front of the results, not the preliminaries.

Unexpected and swift developments occurred. On the same day I received that presidential request, I returned home earlier than usual, thinking about what I would do, knowing I didn't have much time. Although neither the letter nor the visitors indicated a specific deadline, I didn't need further proof of the extortion. Even if the ruthless hawk himself hadn't sent the letter, the extortion was real in one way or another. A threat had to be taken seriously; it concerned my future, my business, my wealth, and all the years I had spent working hard after leaving my original family, sacrificing my feelings and longings to build another world.

When I arrived home, I found my aunt in an unusual state, breathing heavily, gasping, clutching her chest. She had never suffered from heart, chest, or stomach pain before.

People say misfortunes never come alone, and that's exactly what happened to me. For a moment, I thought my early return must have been for another reason I hadn't known. God works in mysterious ways.

I rushed to lay her on the couch in the living room as she struggled to speak, then hurriedly took her to the hospital. Moments later, the doctor gave me the devastating news:

'She's gone. May you live a long life. Her soul has ascended to the heavens.'

I didn't know what to say or do. Is life really this trivial? It brings us here just to break us, then expels us without warning?

I muttered to myself, then sought God's forgiveness and thought about life's distractions. Then, the image of the ruthless hawk flashed in my mind, along with his demand that I pay my 'national duty'—that elusive concept, existing only in torn-up school books and old stories from grandmothers.

Is this really the time for the hawk? I needed to focus on giving my aunt the respect she deserved and handle the necessary arrangements. I had to fight back my tears, my pain, and my grief because she was the last person I truly loved—or had grown attached to, if I were to be precise.

I never thought her end would come so suddenly. My uncle had passed after a long illness, but she had quickly ascended to the heavens. I asked the doctor, who stood before me, perhaps observing my confusion and my unstoppable tears:

'Is there any cause? What happened?'

He replied, moving his stethoscope as if indifferent to what had occurred:

'There's nothing. When fate arrives, no doctor or jinn can stop it.'

I paid the hospital fees and hurried to collect my aunt's body, having brought her in still breathing, even if her heart was aching or she couldn't speak.

Then I became absorbed in the bureaucratic details surrounding death, and there was no real person to stand by me. Yes, dozens, perhaps hundreds, came to me, supporting me to the end. But no one was truly there to help me with genuine kindness, the kind spun by ancient tales, which probably exists only in imagination.

I imagined the president would come to offer his condolences for my aunt's—my mother's—death. But the man didn't appear. Instead, the ruthless hawk was speaking in parliament on the evening of the burial. The mourners talked about his speech, in which he announced that he had allowed the Southerners to hold a referendum on dividing the country if they wished to establish their own nation.

The image of the dark-skinned girl crossed my mind, and I felt a deep loneliness. I remembered my Turkish sister and then forgot everything, thinking only of my aunt and the ruthless hawk's demand. I ignored the people filling the space in front of me, exchanging condolences—'May God have mercy on her soul, may He accept her,' and other comforting words that couldn't alleviate the weight of fate.

Late at night, I was alone in the house where I had once entered as a guest. Too exhausted, I found myself lying in the same room where I had slept for the first time. The lighting was dim, and there were distant sounds, as if coming from my hometown. I was filled with longing for them, and between wakefulness and sleep, I drifted into beautiful worlds, despite my sorrow. I saw my aunt waving to me from afar in a lovely green place, and then I saw my uncle speaking to me in words I understood well but couldn't remember when I woke up in the morning.

Life, despite the exhaustion, pains, and sorrows, was beautiful, though I still feared the ruthless hawk's threats and remained uncertain about what tomorrow would bring.

8

The Escape

In the distant horizon, solutions always loom, and there's always a way out for a person from their predicament. Early in the morning, I called the man with the earring in Turkey. I hadn't spoken to him in a long time. I told him that my aunt had passed away and that I was in the most difficult yet expansive moment of my life. I said to him:

'I'm living in a situation that's hard for me to explain, and I can't predict what's coming. I have no one here.'

I paused for a moment and then told him what I truly intended, that decision that came to me in the early dawn:

'I don't think I'll stay here much longer. This place can no longer bear me.'

He was smart enough to understand what I meant. There was much to say over the phone, but revealing too much could have negative consequences regarding what I had decided. He ended the call by saying:

'From my side, we'll arrange everything for you. Just follow through with what you've decided.'

And no more than a day passed before I had finished many of the accumulated tasks. I didn't concern myself with the issue of the Hawk's demand. I had decided that I would escape with as much victory as possible.

I resolved not to let the past years of my life go to waste. I began tallying up my bank accounts and assets. There was no one I trusted enough in this country to rely on for arranging what remained of my affairs. This was the conclusion of my experience with this place, especially after the highest authority tried to extort me.

Knowing the people who could help me for money and bribes, I had already transferred my wealth into accounts abroad, where the man with the earring had taken care of everything on the other side. I trusted him and had no doubt that he would handle everything as I had decided.

I completed the paperwork for anonymous proxies to manage my remaining businesses, liquidate them, and sell my properties. As long as the money flowed, everything would go smoothly.

I stayed hidden for ten days, with no one knowing where I was. In reality, I was renting a room in an old hotel in the heart of the big city, near my multi-story building. From my hotel room window, I would gaze at the building, remembering how much time and money I had spent to make it stand tall. Today, I was forced to leave it, along with many other things.

It had to happen; there was no other choice in this situation. Once the extortion began, it wouldn't stop. In the past, I paid specific fees or bribes to certain people, but today I was up against the state, the authority, and the law—the Hawk. I couldn't resist forever. The only solution was what I had already thought of.

I escaped across the land border to a neighbouring country and then flew to Istanbul, on my first trip outside the homeland.

My Turkish sister, my cousin, greeted me, apologising that the man with the earring was busy and would meet me later. She received me with great warmth, saying:

'I've been following what's going on there. No one can survive unless they have Moses' staff.'

We talked about my uncle and my aunt, about how they loved that country. She quickly handed me her new book, which she had published less than a month ago. I wasn't particularly interested in its subject, as it dealt with complex issues about Turkey's struggles over its identity in a new era, torn between aligning with Europe and preserving its Eastern heritage. But I forgot that I was about to become a citizen here, perhaps for the rest of my life. I hastened to say:

'I'll read it fully and as soon as possible.'

She gave me a signed copy. She had dedicated it to her father's memory, the uncle who, as she put it, found his unique identity in another place. I told her:

'Today, I may find my own identity here. I'm not sure about the future'

'Don't worry, don't let doubts consume you. Everything will be fine. Rest assured your sister is with you,' she replied.

She embraced me in the large villa's hall, while one of the servants watched us from a distance, as if confirming a betrayal being committed against the great lord in the name of this stranger who had just arrived and whom he had never seen before.

I kissed her strongly, not knowing why I did that. But I couldn't control myself. I held her hand, or perhaps she took mine, I'm not sure. We entered a room draped in purple—the colour I love. We sat beside each other. She rested her head on my shoulder as if she hadn't slept in a long time or was exhausted. She whispered to me softly:

'I've always longed to have a brother like you.'

'I'm here, your brother. Don't think of anyone else who isn't around,' I said.

'I've loved you since I first saw you and since I heard my father speak about you so much,' she told me.

I answered her, feeling something strange stirring in my soul:

'I don't deserve that. I'm just a lost soul without family or country.'

She smiled as she closed her eyes and said:

'That's not true. I could never forget you. My father loved you deeply, and I will always love you. I was always sure you would be by my side one day.'

She gently stroked my cheek, and that small gesture was enough for me to understand it as a touch of pure affection, filled with sincere brotherly love. Nothing else, nothing improper, just a deep human connection.

For minutes, and sometimes, my thoughts would drift in a negative direction, but I felt a sense of discomfort as she insisted on holding me tightly. It was as if she were drunk or battling a strange existential feeling, as though she didn't belong in the same space.

I looked around and asked her:

'Why is your husband late?'

'He's been kind to you. He didn't want to embarrass you. He did what was needed because he respects me, even though we separated long ago.'

This news was both sad and uplifting, and I didn't care much to know the reasons. I wasn't sure what exactly I felt as I held her close while she held me. I savoured the sweetness of her lips, fragrant with the charm of Istanbul and the scent of the Turkish East. I drifted into a distant realm, forgetting myself. I must have fallen asleep beside her. I don't know what happened next.

…The important thing, my son…

Come, let me show you something. Take this pouch. Never let go of it, for perhaps its owner will return one day.

---

*Available worldwide from Amazon
and all good bookstores*

www.mtp.agency

www.facebook.com/mtp.agency

@mtp_agency

www.ingramcontent.com/pod-product-compliance
Lightning Source LLC
LaVergne TN
LVHW041628060526
838200LV00040B/1487